74

SECRET PRAGUE

Martin Stejskal

JonGlez

We have taken great pleasure in drawing up *Secret Prague* and hope that through its guidance you will, like us, continue to discover unusual, hidden or little-known aspects of the city. Descriptions of certain places are accompanied by thematic sections highlighting historical details or anecdotes as an aid to understanding the city in all its complexity.

Secret Prague also draws attention to the multitude of details found in places that we may pass every day without noticing. These are an invitation to look more closely at the urban landscape and, more generally, a means of seeing our own city with the curiosity and attention that we often display while travelling elsewhere …

Comments on this guidebook and its contents, as well as information on places wc may not have mentioned, are more than welcome and will enrich future editions.

Don't hesitate to contact us:

• Éditions Jonglez, 17, boulevard du Roi, 78000 Versailles, France
• E-mail: info@jonglezpublishing.com

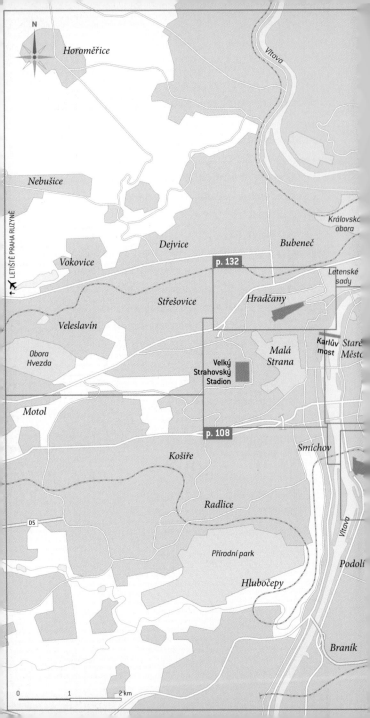

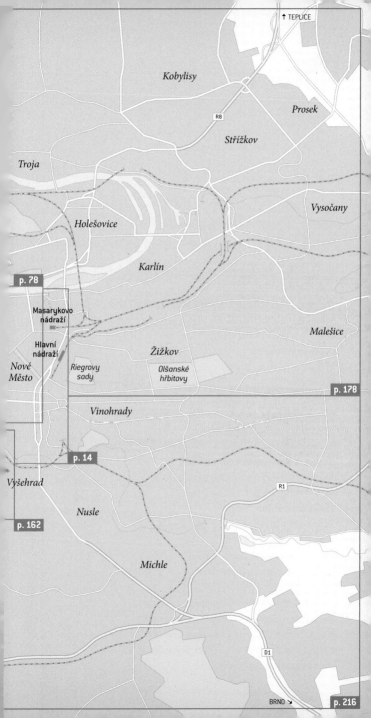

↑ TEPLICE

Kobylisy

Prosek

R8

Střížkov

Troja

Vysočany

Holešovice

Karlín

p. 78

Masarykovo
nádraží

Malešice

Hlavní
nádraží

Žižkov

Nové
Město

Riegrovy
sady

Olšanské
hřbitovy

p. 178

Vinohrady

p. 14

Vyšehrad

R1

p. 162

Nusle

Michle

D1

BRNO ↘ p. 216

CONTENTS

NOVÉ MĚSTO

CONTENTS

MALÁ STRANA (LESSER TOWN)

HRADČANY (CASTLE)

VYŠEHRAD

CONTENTS

OUTSIDE THE CENTRE - NORTH

OUTSIDE THE CENTRE - SOUTH

INDEX

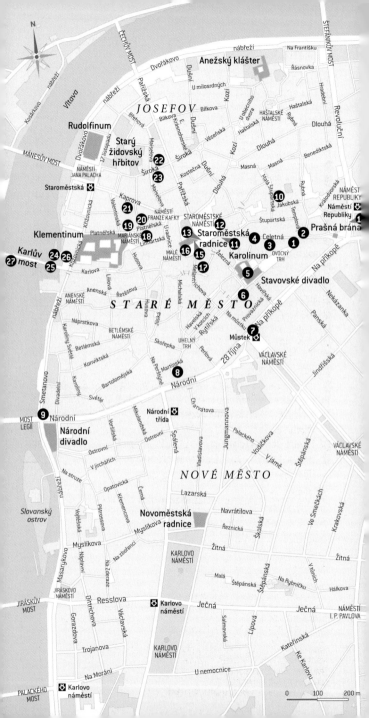

STARÉ MĚSTO - JOSEFOV

THE ROYAL WAY: FROM THE CLASSICAL TO THE ALCHEMICAL

Prague, like other European cities such as Paris, was laid out according to the orientation of sunset and sunrise at the solstices and equinoxes. This obvious east–west axis, established in the distant past, runs past the royal residence at the castle and the Ungelt, the commercial centre in the Old Town. The axis is part of the route taken by the relics of St Wenceslas, patron saint of Bohemia, from Stará Boleslav, where they were kept, to the "hill of the dolphin or sea pig" (the castle).

Emperor Charles IV, who had established a detailed ritual for coronation processions along this route, had already given a specific meaning to this emergent axis when he assigned it a key role in the so-called Royal Way as part of his plans to reconstruct the Old Town and found the New Town.

As the European capital of esotericism and alchemy in the 17th century (see p. 140), Prague also turned this Royal Way into an immense allegory in hermetic terms of the path to discovering the philosopher's stone.

Its many twists and turns, adventurous stories, and especially its vast number of personal symbols encountered by the alchemist during his journey, have their analogies – here on doors and gateways, there on corbelled roofs and house signs.

In the light of this hermetic perspective, the Royal Way to the castle may be considered as having a double meaning: *exoteric* as this was the route followed by the coronation procession of a new king; *esoteric* because it leads by numerous significant symbols directly to the west, towards the Evening Star (see p. 194).

The Royal Way enters the Old Town from the east, at the Powder Gate, which symbolises the threshold of the alchemical way (see p. 23), and continues at the junction of Celetná and Ovocný trh (Fruit Market), near the ancient temple and the House of the Black Madonna, the source of primary matter for the Great Work: this is the beginning of the alchemical path (see p. 23).

The route from Celetná to Old Town Square and Karlova Street passes through a forest of symbols that deal allegorically with aspects of the alchemical process: the House at the Golden Angel, with a winged spirit holding a laurel wreath, recalls the reward that will come to whoever perseveres with this difficult philosophical path.

Next comes the House of the Black Sun, reminiscent of the decomposition or putrefaction of the nigredo (blackness) stage of the Great Work. Similarly, the House at the Two Golden Bears recalls that, as matter can be controlled, the bear, too, can be mastered (see p. 55).

Further along the road, the House at the Golden Wheel (see p. 32) and the medallions At the Stone Lamb (see p. 44) are a reminder that the alchemy is fully under way. The *sgraffiti* of the Virgin's gushing breast milk on the House at the Minute symbolise the beginning of the second stage of the work: albedo (whiteness or purification).

On Charles Bridge, the gestures of the row of saints clearly show the traveller the way to the west. St Christopher here is carrying an increasingly heavy burden (newly created gold) towards the glow of the setting Sun (see p. 77).

Entering Malá Strana (House at the Two Suns, p. 114), the road forks right towards the castle (glory and fame of the exoteric way) and left towards the Star Summer Palace (Hvězda), the final step on the esoteric path (elevation and spiritual enlightenment, p. 194).

On the final stretch, the House at the Golden Apple symbolises the philosopher's stone, which is now very close (see p. 113).

The other route is more direct: it runs due west through Strahov above the royal residence, where the Evening Star gleams above the horizon – the promise of success in the journey to the Great Work.

Above Úvoz Street the two towers of Strahov Monastery stand like spiritual sentinels: between them, the route passes (next to the oldest Czech centre of divinity, Břevnov Monastery) on its way to the Star Summer Palace, whose site – seemingly so remote from the city centre – can perhaps now be explained (see p. 194).

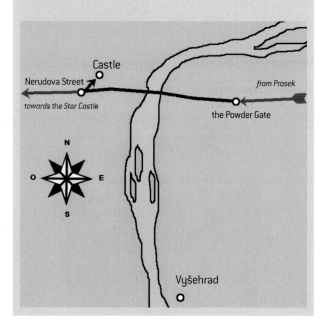

For more information on alchemy, its origins and symbolism, see p. 19.

ALCHEMY

Most religious orders of the Middle Ages and the Renaissance considered *alchemy* (from the Coptic term *Allah-Chemia*, or divine chemistry) as the *Art of the Holy Spirit* or *Royal Art* of the divine creation of the world and man. It was connected to Orthodox Catholic doctrine.

The followers of this art divided it into two principal forms. *Spiritual alchemy* exclusively concerns the inspiration of the soul, transforming the impure elements of the body in the refined states of spiritual consciousness, which is also called the *Way of the Repentants*. *Laboratory alchemy*, called the *Way of the Philosophers*, reproduces the alchemical universe of the transmutation of nature's impure elements into noble metals, such as silver and gold, in the laboratory. These two alchemical practices are generally followed in combination, thus becoming the *Way of the Humble*, where the humility is that of man faced with the grandeur of the universe reproduced in the laboratory (in Latin *labor + oratorium*); the alchemy of the (interior) soul is expressed exteriorly in the laboratory. Those who practise *Laboratory alchemy* with the sole purpose of finding silver and gold, and thus neglect the essential aspects of the betterment of the soul, will fail and become *charlatans*, who might have a wide-ranging culture but certainly not the required moral qualities. To avoid becoming a *charlatan* (it was this heretic form that was condemned by the Church), followers must balance the heart and soul, culture and moral qualities, penitence and humility, to become a true philosopher.

THE 12 STEPS OF THE ALCHEMICAL GREAT WORK AND THEIR SYMBOLS

The alchemical Great Work can be expressed as a series of laboratory operations on the substance of the chemical elements of Nature, eliminating their physical impurities (Death), purifying and reuniting them (Resurrection), with mercury and sulphur (Soul and Spirit) acting on salt (base matter). Thus the volatile elements fixed in purified matter will gradually, over the 12 steps, create the philosopher's stone, which is synonymous with the Illumination of Matter by the release of the Spirit imprisoned within it.

These 12 interconnected steps are briefly outlined here for those who may be unfamiliar with hermetic thought and language. They are carried out in three distinct stages, each divided into four steps.

Nigredo (blackness) – dissolution and putrefaction of matter

Calcination – this is the purification of the original solid matter by fire, without decreasing its water content (referred to as "Dew"), so that it chars without turning to ashes. Its symbol is the *lion*, which indicates strength and solar light, as shown in alchemical iconography by the operator who maintains the balance of fire and water. This step is also symbolised by the *dragon* in flames.

Solution or *Dissolution* – the solid matter is transformed, reduced to the liquid state and dispersed in this solvent: the "philosophical dissolution" where the water is mercury itself, which dissolves the essence of the differentiated chemical element by integrating it with its undifferentiated original state, the raw material. The symbol of this step is a *crowned man* (follower of the "royal art") *bathing in a lake* (the "mercurial waters") and expresses an internal leap of faith.

Separation – just as the Spirit is distinct from the Soul, mercury is separated from its sulphur component, and when heated to the correct temperature coagulates by a secret process (*Secretum Secretorum*) only known to alchemists. This is a form of dividing line between alchemy and chemistry, metaphorically capturing a sunray inside a glass flask (or "philosophical egg"), condensing it and hermetically sealing it by heating the flask on the fire.

The Earth – the solid element – remains at the bottom, while the Spirit rises. Once this step is successfully completed, a star (the "rainbow" or "peacock's tail") can be seen forming in the flask. This stage is marked in alchemical iconography by the *shining star*, also by the *knight's sword*.

Putrefaction – heat kills the solid bodies in the flask and they decay: a dark blackish colour then forms, represented by two *crows* (one indicating calcination and the other putrefaction), or by the *Grim Reaper with his scythe*, and sometimes by a *Moor* or simply a *decapitated and blackened head*.

Albedo (whiteness) – purification of matter by the "liquid" substance

Conjunction – aware of their separate existence, the Soul and the Spirit, mercury and sulphur, are reunited. This operation is carried out in the same tightly sealed flask. Because this step represents the "hermetic wedding", it is symbolised by a *King* (Spirit, Sun) and a *Queen* (Soul, Moon) with their hands clasped together.

Coagulation or *Congelation* – in this step, an off-white colour appears in the flask, gently heated to cause the change in the matter. This is the cooling process which solidifies a liquid: the previously dissolved solid reappears and the solvent evaporates. It signifies the return of the duly cleansed element to the Earth, as in the resurrection of the body, and is represented by a *King bearing a sceptre rising from his tomb*.

Cibation – this step is the addition of the chemical elements needed to feed the dry matter in the crucible, represented by a *dragon* framed by the Sun and Moon.

Sublimation – in this step, matter becomes spiritual and mind becomes matter, i.e. what is fixed evaporates and what is volatile is fixed, but these two processes are interdependent, otherwise it is impossible to vaporise (disappear) or fix (solidify). The predominant role is once again that of the element Air, the principle of sublimation of the Spirit and of Matter, because this is where vapour solidifies and dry matter rises on the application of heat. This step is said to last 40 days. The symbolic iconography may equally well show a *dove descending into the crucible* or an *eagle rising from the crucible*. Other representations are that of an *old man lying prone* with a dove hovering over him and an eagle perched on his stomach, while above him are the astrological symbols of the seven classical planets (Sun, Moon, Mars, Mercury, Jupiter, Venus, Saturn).

Rubedo (redness) – when the philosopher's stone is created

Fermentation – this is the reaction of an organic body to matter that causes it to decompose, as well as the chemical transformation accompanied by natural effervescence from fermentation or a similar process. However, in alchemy it was customary to add gold to activate the reaction, given that "Nature reproduces from Nature herself". The symbols of fermentation are images of the *hermaphrodite* and the *wine barrel*, sometimes replaced by the figure of the *god Bacchus or Dionysus*.

Exaltation – this step is identical to sublimation, a kind of resublimation or spiritual exaltation which is at the same time chemical, marked by the presence of gold and mercury. It is indicated by images of the *god Jupiter with his arrows of fire* and the *mermaid Melusine* signifying the "mercury of the philosophers".

Multiplication – in this step, further heating the matter increases its power without increasing its quantity. This matter becomes the "powder of projection" required for the transmutation of base metals into pure gold. This is when the philosopher's stone starts to appear in its primitive form. The Bible describes this process of multiplication in Christ's Miracle of the Loaves, and the iconic allegories are the *lake* and its waters of "eternal youth" and a *goat standing on a mount*.

Projection – this is the final application of the philosopher's stone as it was habitually employed, such as in the transmutation of base metal, by throwing the stone or its "powder of projection" onto the molten metal to turn it into gold. Given a bright red or purple colouring, the philosopher's stone – issue of the sublimated salt which is the quintessence of matter – is represented by a *crowned Child*. Descendant of the King and Queen, the Sun and the Moon, sulphur and mercury, he is the divine Crown Prince, dressed sometimes in immaculate white, sometimes in luminous purple. He represents the revelation of Spirit over Matter, and therefore the illumination of the body by the Divine Essence, the ultimate goal of true alchemists. This step is also represented by the *hedgehog* and the *sacred chalice* that the knights of old on their spiritual quest named the *Holy Grail*.

SYMBOLISM OF THE HOUSE OF THE BLACK ❶ MADONNA

Celetná 43
• Metro: Náměstí republiky

> *Blackness,
> the first phase
> of the alchemical
> process*

At the entrance to the Old Town, through the Powder Gate (see box below), the House of the Black Madonna (dům U černé Matky Boží) at the junction of Celetná and Ovocný trh, takes its name from the sculpture on the corner.

The importance of the Black Madonna lies in her telluric nature, resulting from an intimate connection with the depths of the earth. She occupies a prominent place near the Temple, the former residence of the Knights Templar – Christian knights who helped to spread the cult of the Black Madonna in Europe.

By her prominent position almost at the beginning of the Royal Way (see p. 16), the Black Madonna also personifies "nigredo" – the first phase of the alchemical process also known as putrefaction that transforms coarse elements into subtle, golden ones (indicated by the gold on the Madonna's mantle). The mantle, which not all Black Madonna statues have, is a reminder in this case that the wisdom embodied by the Madonna is hidden – it is only revealed to those who put in the necessary work, symbolised by the Great Work of alchemy.

The Madonna was set up here in 1911–12, when Josef Gočár constructed Prague's finest Cubist building on the site of a house that belonged to the Granovský Knights and already featured the Madonna. The building now houses the Museum of Czech Cubism.

The Madonna has always been protected by a grille, which is why the house is also known as U zlaté mříže (At the Golden Grille). Since 1997, the statue behind the grille is a copy: the original forms part of the exhibition devoted to the Hermetic Magnum Opus in the basement of U kameného zvonu, the house next to the Church of Our Lady before Týn (Old Town Square).

POWDER GATE: ON THE THRESHOLD OF THE ALCHEMICAL PATH

The Powder Gate (Prašná brána) signals the entrance to the Old Town. Interestingly, in Czech, the word *prach* (powder) and *práh* (threshold) are very similar. For some, the fact that gunpowder was stored there from the 18th century also recalls, in alchemical terms, the pulverising of matter in preparation for the Great Work.

For more on Black Madonnas and their significance, see the following double-page spread.

BLACK VIRGINS: VESTIGES OF PRE-CHRISTIAN RELIGIONS?

The Black Virgins are effigies of the Virgin Mary (sculptures, icons, paintings) which, for the most part, were created between the eleventh and fourteenth centuries. Their name refers quite simply to their dark colour.

Around 500 of them have been counted, mainly around the Mediterranean basin. Usually found in churches, some of them have been the object of major pilgrimages.

According to the Roman Catholic Church, there is no theological basis for the colour of these Virgins, although some experts have pointed to the passage in the Song of Songs (1:5): "*Nigra sum sed formosa*" which can be translated as "I am black but beautiful".

Some other very simple reasons have been proposed to explain this black colouring: the colour of the material used (ebony, mahogany, or a dark local wood) or deposits of soot from votive candles. But the importance that this colour has taken over time (some images have even been repainted black during restorations) leads to the belief that a deeper force is at work.

Thus, for some, the colour of the Black Virgin is a reminder that the Virgin, like the Catholic religion in general, did not become established *ex nihilo*, but replaced other ancient faiths in Western Europe: the Mithraic cult (for more details on this fascinating cult which was fundamental in creating a European identity, see *Secret Rome* in this series of guides),

Mother-goddess cults, the cult of the Egyptian goddess Isis bearing Horus in her arms, etc.

In these archaic contexts, tribute was often rendered to the Mother goddess, symbol of fertility, gestation, procreation, regeneration, and renewal of life in general, on which the peasantry relied to ensure a bountiful harvest.

As the Christian religion began to affirm itself, the Virgin, mother of Jesus, son of God the Creator, thus became associated with this Mother goddess.

In symbolic terms, the black colour of the Virgin naturally evokes that of the virgin earth as well as the maternal/regenerative side of life in the sense that feminine procreation takes place in the (dark/black) depths of the woman's uterus. And her dark colour may also have brought her closer to the peasants whose own skin darkened from working out in the fields in the sun.

So it is therefore no accident if similar inscriptions are found on certain statues of Isis as on many of the Black Virgins: *"Virgini pariturae"* (to the Virgin who will give birth).

Finally, although many of the Black Virgins are associated with miracles, it is interesting to note that these events are usually linked to the beginning of a new cycle or a new era, thus respecting the image of the Virgin as the giver of life, above all else.

AT THE GOLDEN ANGEL   ❷

Celetná 29
• Metro: Náměstí republiky

*An angel
for company
on the Royal Way ...*

On the Royal Way (see p. 16) at No. 29 Celetná, the house known as U zlatého anděla (At the Golden Angel) bears the golden figure of a winged spirit holding aloft a laurel wreath in his right hand as if preparing to crown a victor. (This is a copy – the original has been moved to the Municipal Museum.)

His left hand holds a horn of plenty filled with fruit, a symbol of the promise made at the beginning of this difficult philosophical path to bestow the laurel wreath on the one who persists and succeeds. At the same time, this is the first expression of the hidden science: not many people spot Mercury's winged caduceus under the fruit. So from the start of this route we are greeted by the *servus fugitivus* (flying or winged servant), the *paredros* or familiar spirit who henceforth accompanies the visitor.

AT THE WHITE PEACOCK

Celetná 10
• Metro: Náměstí republiky

> **The peacock's tail, an alchemical symbol**

On the Royal Way (see p. 16), the house at No. 10 Celetná – known as U bílého páva (At the White Peacock) – is a modern residence although the site has been so named since the early 16th century.

In antiquity the peacock was associated with the goddess Hera, wife of Jupiter, but was also a symbol of the Sun because of the wide spread of its tail, similar to the solar disc. In esoteric traditions, "the peacock's tail", with all the colours of the rainbow, leads to a single colour, white, which embodies all colours.

So we move on to the second phase of alchemy: after nigredo (the Black Madonna) comes albedo, the change to whiteness.

HIDDEN SYMBOLISM AT THE BLACK SUN ❹

Celetná 8
• Metro: Náměstí republiky

> *From Black Madonna to Black Sun ...*

At No. 8 Celetná, at the entrance to the Gothic house U černého slunce (At the Black Sun), the sign of the Sun shines out of an ornate Baroque cartouche.

Although this is one of the best-known houses in Prague, its significance is less clear.

Sited on the Royal Way (see p. 16), it also has a hermetic meaning: as the Sun is traditionally associated with gold, the Black Sun in alchemical treatises is an allegory of the raw material in its original, unworked state.

The Black Sun also owes its name to the idea that it contains so much illuminating power (after the various alchemical operations, realisation of the Great Work is also and above all a spiritual enlightenment) that it obscures

the vision of ordinary mortals. Revelation is only bearable for the great initiates, illuminated by divine wisdom: for others, such as Cambyses the King of Persia, who wished to see its face in the Egyptian desert, madness and destruction would surely follow.

This cartouche confirms that we are still at the stage that alchemists refer to as nigredo, into which we entered with the Black Madonna at the corner of Celetná (see p. 23).

There are two other houses called At the Black Sun in Prague, but they have no sign: one is at No. 9 Mostecká Street and the other at No. 13 Všehrdova Street.

GREEN MAN OF KAROLINUM

Ovocný trh 3, Praha 1
• Metro: Můstek – A

❺

> **A reminder
> of the need
> to respect nature**

A curious representation of a man with branches sticking out of his mouth and his head covered with foliage (see below) can be found on a number of Prague buildings.

Although the origins of this figure are pagan, similar examples began to appear on the capitals of Gothic churches and cathedrals, even sometimes on secular buildings. It became very fashionable in the late 19th century, occurring throughout Europe (particularly in the United Kingdom) as well as Thailand, India and Nepal.

This striking figure is a symbol of rebirth and new beginnings, a reminder of the perpetual cycle renewed each spring.

Its meaning is associated with Silvanus, the spirit of the forest, and Faunus, with whom he is often identified.

There are two types of Green Man: the first induces fear (almost exclusively, the medieval examples) and represents a King of the Forest. In this sense, the figure is a reminder of the need to respect nature and its cycles. The second type is that of the Green Men who appeared primarily in the Renaissance and

the Baroque period and usually correspond to a mask of leaves and a symmetrical tangle of vegetation.

In Anglo-Saxon folklore, the Green Man is often associated with a spirit called Jack-in-the-Green. In the Czech lands, the town of Lanškroun has a legend telling of a local forest spectre known as Green Jack (Zelený Honza).

OTHER SCULPTURES OF GREEN MEN IN PRAGUE:
– on St Vitus Cathedral in Hrad any, which has several Green Men, carved during the restoration of the late 19th century;
– at the Church of St Haštal in the Old Town (eight Green Men);
– on the Powder Tower (on the corners of the tower: two Green Men looking towards Celetná);
– in the arcade of Týnská school, Old Town Square (on the keystone);
– on D m u Kamenného zvonu (Chapel of the House), Old Town Square (on the keystone).

AT THE GOLDEN WHEEL ⑥

Rytířská 18
• Metro: Můstek

The alchemical fire wheel

Although the sign of the golden wheel on U zlatého cola (At the Golden Wheel), a house dating from 1787, is well known, not many people are aware of its true meaning.

On the façade of the house, two angels can be seen slightly raising the lid of a tomb with two unrecognizable heads peeking out. On the second floor, the eight-spoked golden wheel after which the house is named is bordered by two cartouches: one of Athena surmounted by the severed head of Medusa, and on the right a bust of Mercury with a caduceus.

The site of the house, close to the main road, means that an alchemical explanation is likely.

In the alchemical process, after the preparatory steps, the matter is placed in a special recipient and loaded into the furnace (athanor) where the transformation of the elements can begin. The wheel of the elements then starts to slowly rotate with the help of the secret fire. From this moment, no one must stop or slow the rotation. This phase is known as the "Fire Wheel" and its alchemical symbol (✹) closely resembles the house sign.

This fire is a Kabbalistic symbol of the mnemonic chant *Rota* which, when rapidly and constantly repeated, reveals the secret link with the book of books – the Tarot.

It is the rotation that continually changes the components of the Earth's igneous material (fire) into air, then from air to water and back to terrestrial matter. This is why the wheel is protected by Athena, goddess of wisdom, armed with a spear that with a glance from Medusa can ward off any inauspicious circumstances, and Hermes, who exchanged his helmet with that of Mars in preparation for a struggle.

AT THE GOLDEN HIVE

28 října 15
• Metro: Můstek

Allegory of the esoteric Rosicrucians

Surmounting the façade of the house known as U zlatého úlu (At the Golden Hive), a semicircular high relief shows a great golden hive set on a rock, with bees flying in and out.

All around is rolling countryside where trees and roses grow.

In the sky, partially covered by clouds, a golden Sun shines to the left, while lower down to the right is a crescent Moon in the ascendant.

Although for many local people this is an ancient symbol of thrift, in fact it recalls almost identical scenes in many Rosicrucian illustrations published in the first half of the 17th century.

Robert Fludd's treatise *Clavis Philosophiae et Alchymiae* (1623), for example, depicts a rose in the centre of a cross, towards which the bee is flying from the hive. The Latin inscription around the rose reads *Dat rosa mel apibus* (The rose gives honey to the bee).

Symbolically, under the protection of the two main protagonists of the alchemical Great Work (the Sun and the Moon), the hive represents the Lodge where Rosicrucians carry out their work and the bees are members of the Order, the whole being an allegory of Fraternity and Mutual Aid.

For more on the Rosecrucians, see the following double-page spread.

ROSICRUCIANS: AN ORDER OF ESOTERIC AND MYSTICAL CHRISTIANITY

The name of this esoteric Order comes from that of a German elder

who lived around 1460 and was known as Christian Rosenkreutz (Christian Rose-Cross). Together with twelve disciples deeply versed in Christian mysticism, he set up an Order dedicated to the study of the religious and scientific learning of the day. Having established themselves in the south of Europe, these scholar-mystics came into contact with the spiritual and cultural learning of the Islamic world – in particular, with Sufism. These contacts remained close for a long time, thus creating a spiritual link between East and West. Tradition has it that the Rosicrucians had superhuman powers thanks to their profound knowledge of hermetism and alchemy; that they knew how to create the philosopher's stone; that they spoke directly to God, Christ, the saints and the angels; and that through these contacts they learned divine wisdom and the secrets of immortality.

Their reputation for supernatural miracle-working powers continues to this day, without it being clear where reality ends and fantasy begins. The Rosicrucians very quickly faded into anonymity from the fifteenth century onwards, becoming a secret society. Indeed, no new member was accepted before the death of an existing member – thus keeping the numbers equal to 1+12, on the model of Christ and his twelve Apostles. In 1614 a work written in German (with the Latin title *Fama Fraternitatis*) was attributed to Christian Rosenkreutz, though its actual author was the theologian Johannes Valentinus Andreae (1586–1654), who was supposedly the spokesman of the Order of Rosicrucians and signed himself as its "Grand Master". He describes the origins, history and mission of the Rosicrucians, who were striving to restore primordial Christianity and rid the Church of the secular vices to which it had fallen prey.

When Freemasonry evolved in the eighteenth century, it embraced Rosicrucianism, establishing in 1761 the 18th degree of *Prince of the Rose Cross* or *Knight of the Pelican* – a strictly Christian division (the bird being a Christian symbol of charity, abnegation and sacrifice).

Several scholars – such as the English physician and philosopher Robert Fludd in his 1629 *Summum Bonum* – distinguish between the Rose Cross and Rosicrucianism, with a further distinction later being made between Rose-Cross Masons and former Freemasons. The bases for this distinction are as follows:

Rose Cross refers to he who has achieved spiritual illumination, the Master who knows and applies divine mysteries because he is spiritually and inwardly in the image of Christ, the Supreme Being. Here, the emblem of the Rose Cross represents complete Enlightenment, the spirit (Rose) which enlightens and guides matter (Cross).

Rosicrucian: the disciple who has chosen to adopt the discipline that leads to the higher level of Rose Cross. The symbol of the Rose Cross here symbolises the love (Rose) and the perfection (Cross) that are to be achieved.

Rose-Cross Mason: this is the symbolic initiate who has achieved the 18th degree of Freemasonry. In this case, the Rose Cross placed at the centre of a set-square and pair of compasses represents the perfection and justice of Christ's message.

GARGOYLE OF A BOY

Church of St Martin-in-the-Wall
Martinská
• Metro: Můstek; Tram: 22 or 9

> *A wretched boy turned to stone?*

Having had the Old Town wall built around it (hence the name), the Church of St Martin in the Wall is in a quiet and gloomy neighbourhood, linked to Martinská Street by a narrow alley.

Look up and on one of the pillars you can see the figure of a small boy lying down and peering over the edge, like the gargoyles of Gothic cathedrals.

According to legend, the boy is a hooligan who stole eggs from pigeons' nests, although some say he was apprenticed to a roofer and that from his vantage point on the roof he mocked a priest giving the last rites.

The boy comes to the same end in both versions: as punishment, he is said to have been turned to stone.

St Martin in the Wall was built between 1178 and 1187 in the then village of Újezd and was consequently known as Újezd-St-Martin. A little later, when the Old Town walls were built in the first half of the 13th century, the village was divided into two. Most of it remained outside the walls in what is now the New Town; the smaller section, along with the church, was integrated with the Old Town.

The south side of the church became part of the ramparts and nearby was a gateway named after St Martin. Of the original Romanesque church there remains only the main nave, which features several Romanesque architectural details.

The interior was probably decorated with Romanesque murals. During the reign of Charles IV, after 1350, the nave was raised and a wall was built near the south-west corner. A presbytery was also built to a square plan, thereby increasing the surface area of the church.

For centuries, a cemetery surrounded the church. Its existence is commemorated in a plaque by the Brokoff family of sculptors (18th century). The best-known member of this family, F. M. Brokoff (1688–1731), known for his statues on Charles Bridge, is also buried here. Some old tombstones have been preserved inside the church.

PAINTING OF AN ABSINTHE DRINKER

Café Slavia
Národní třída
• Metro: Národní třída; Tram: 9, 22, Národní divadlo stop

I n the superb and celebrated Art Deco Café Slavia is a lovely painting by Viktor Oliva, *The Absinthe Drinker* (1901), which has graced the café since the 1920s.

> **"The Green Fairy", another name for absinthe**

It shows an absinthe drinker confronted by a "green fairy", which brings to mind another name for this drink.

Viktor Oliva (1861–1928) belonged to the "Parisian Bohemians", as the Czech artists (from Bohemia) who lived in Paris in the late 19th and early 20th centuries were known. It was in Paris that Oliva discovered the joys of absinthe.

He was strongly influenced by his artist friends, Art Nouveau practitioners such as Alfons Mucha and Luděk Marold.

Café Slavia opened in 1863 and became a traditional meeting place for artists including Franz Kafka, Rainer Maria Rilke, Nobel Prize for Literature laureate Jaroslav Seifert, and composers such as Bedřich Smetana and Antonín Dvořák.

ABSINTHE IN BOHEMIA

Absinthe became popular in Bohemia in the 1880s, notably because of Czech artists such as Viktor Oliva, who had discovered the drink during his stay in Paris. Since 1915, Bohemia has been a producer of absinthe.

There are two types of absinthe: the French version, sometimes referred to as the real absinthe, and the East European version (called Czech or Bohemian), which is often blue in colour.

The difference lies in the production method.

Real absinthe is made by macerating wormwood, aniseed, fennel (the so-called "Holy Trinity") and other plants in alcohol, followed by distillation and colouring.

Czech absinthe uses fewer herbs and is filtered after distillation, hence it is very bitter compared with real absinthe.

Hill's distillery, founded in the south of the country in 1920, relaunched the production of Czech absinthe in the 1990s.

A THIEF'S SHRIVELLED HAND

Church of St James Major
Malá Štupartská 635/6
• Open daily 9.30am–12 noon; 2pm–4pm
• Metro: Náměstí Republiky

Set a Virgin to catch a thief ...

In the porch of the Church of St James Major (Jakub Větší), to the right of the entrance, a startling mummified relic hangs from a chain.

The associated legend is that, one day, when a thief broke into the church and tried to steal valuable objects around the statue of the Virgin, she grabbed his wrist and squeezed so hard that his forearm had to be cut off to release him.

It was then exhibited to all and sundry as a warning, and is still there to this day.

BURIED ALIVE

The left aisle of the church also contains the Baroque tomb of Count Vratislav of Mitrovice, with a celebrated sculpture by F. M. Brokoff and B. Fischer von Erlach. The figure of the count is shown surrounded by allegories of Glory, Fame, Saturn and Contemplation. It is said that Count Vratislav was accidently buried alive when he was simply unconscious, and he came round in his coffin. When the tomb was opened later, the coffin lid had been removed and the dead man was lying curled up in a corner of the vault.

The Church of Saint James Major is the largest religious edifice in Prague after St Vitus Cathedral. The façade is decorated with a rich Baroque composition in stucco and the high altar niche contains a Gothic Pietà to which 60 miracles are attributed.

MEDALLIONS AT THE STONE LAMB

🄬

Staroměstské náměstí 551/1
• Metro: Staroměstská

A hidden gem of hermetic architecture

To the left of the entrance to Celetná in Old Town Square, the house U kamenného beranka (At the Stone Lamb) is also sometimes referred to as U jednorožce (At the Unicorn), as the lamb featuring in the bas-relief has a curved horn rather like a unicorn.

This house on the Royal Way (see p. 16) is a hidden gem of hermetic architecture.

In Rudolf II's time it is thought to have belonged to Tadeáš Hájek z Hájků, whom the emperor entrusted with the task of assessing foreign alchemists who were flocking to the city, attracted by his passion for the esoteric disciplines.

Deciphering the symbols carefully, note the richly decorated capitals on the pillars of the gate, which date from the Renaissance.

On the left capital is the Moon, represented as a sickle with a human face turned towards the centre, opposite the Sun, represented by a solar disk with a human face.

On the right capital, the medallion to the left shows a jester's head in profile with a sickle-shaped cap, donkey's ears and three little bells; the medallion to the right shows a pig's head (or a hedgehog's) in profile and a barrel with three embedded hoops.

In alchemy, the jester (or fool) symbolizes Mercury (the principle that corresponds to what is passive, cold, malleable, volatile and female); the hedgehog is the symbol of sulphur, the principle that is active, hot, hard and masculine.

On the left capital, the Sun (gold) and Moon (silver) also correspond to the two fundamental principles of alchemy in action: Sulphur and Mercury.

The surprising construction style of the gate's pillars, in the shape of an X, symbolises the role of the spiritual mediator who completes the alchemist's work.

Other alchemical symbols are also visible: the leaves of the gall oak (which symbolise the secret language of the alchemist), women's work and children's games (in Latin, *opus mulierum* and *ludus puerorum*, reminiscent of processes in the preparation of matter as described in alchemical writings), satyrs astride wild boars, and so on.

Physicist Albert Einstein lived in this house in the early 20th century.

PRAGUE MERIDIAN

Staroměstské náměstí (Old Town Square)
• Metro: Staroměstská

High noon

Although thousands of locals and tourists alike pass through Prague's Old Town Square each day, they may not notice a brass strip running along the cobbles near the Jan Hus monument.

At one end of the strip is inscribed: *meridianus quo olim tempus pragense dirigebatur* (the meridian by which Prague time used to be determined).

This strip does in fact mark the location of the Prague Meridian (14° 25' 17"), by which it was possible to read the time: as in Rome and Paris,* the Marian column that once stood in the square cast a shadow on the ground that moved with the sun. By analysing the position of the shadow over the years, high noon can be determined.

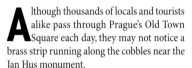

Prague's Marian column was erected in 1650 in gratitude to the Virgin Mary when Swedish troops left the city. Surrounded with statues by Czech sculptor Jan Jiří Bendl, the column was pulled down in 1918 by an angry mob who considered it to be linked to the hated Habsburg rule.

*For more information on meridians in this series of guidebooks, see the Place de la Concorde obelisk in *Secret Paris* and the Vatican obelisk in *Secret Rome*.

The original site of the Marian column is marked by five paving stones in the square.

WHITE CROSSES IN OLD TOWN SQUARE

Staroměstské náměstí (Old Town Square)
• Metro: Staroměstská

27 crosses for 27 martyrs

The white paving stones in the form of 27 crosses near the Town Hall, Old Town Square, commemorate the site of the scaffolding where 27 Czech noblemen (3 lords, 7 knights and 17 burghers) were executed on 21 June 1621 as leaders of the Protestant uprising.

These executions were the culmination of a series of events that began with the defenestration of three Catholic aldermen at Prague Castle on 23 May 1618 and ended in the defeat of the nobles' armies at the Battle of White Mountain on 8 November 1620.

Their deaths were only one consequence of the failed rebellion. Another was that the Czech crown passed to the Habsburgs, a hegemony that was to last some 300 years.

A further important consequence was the return to Roman Catholicism, stimulating a great wave of emigration from Protestant Bohemia, mainly by the intelligentsia, and conversion to Catholicism for those who stayed (see also Symbols of executed nobles, p. 116)

MODERN BAS-RELIEFS AT MUNICIPAL HOUSE ⑭

Obecní dům, Náměstí republiky
• Metro: Náměstí republiky

I f you look up at the first-floor façade of Municipal House (Obecní dům), you will see some magnificent sculptures of allegorical masks with the attributes of Science, Art and Industry on the arches of the 15 semicircular windows. The sculptor is Karel Novák.

A pilot's helmet

Above the last window is the head of a man wearing a flying helmet and goggles, probably an allegory of the Automobile, Motorcycling or Aviation as Municipal House was built in the years 1905–12 when such activities were growing in popularity. Also around this time, the pioneer of Czech aviation Jan Kašpar made the first plane flight in Bohemia (1910).

THE SECRET OF THE ASTRONOMICAL CLOCK ⓯

Staroměstská radnice (Old Town Hall)
Staroměstské náměstí (Old Town Square)
• Metro: Staroměstská

> *A mechanism that gave rise to mathematical modelling*

Built around 1410 by master clockmaker Mikuláš of Kadaň to the plans of Jan Ondřej (also known as Jan Šindel), Prague's famous astronomical clock is a masterpiece of precision engineering. The plaque commemorating its creator is to the left under the lower dial.

A mass of information can be gleaned from the clock faces: classical time in Roman numerals, introduced to Bohemia in 1547; traditional Bohemian time in Gothic numerals, counted from sunset; sidereal (stellar) time; the position of the Sun on the ecliptic; the path and phases of the Moon; the days of the month and feast days, even movable feasts such as Easter, etc. However, another remarkable and little-known feature of the clock is hidden from view: a system of gearwheels that chimes from 1 to 24 times during each full turn.

The small wheel is divided into sections of varying lengths in the ratio 1, 2, 3, 4, 3, 2 (see diagram below). While rotating, it engages with a large toothed wheel with 24 notches on its outer circumference, where the distance between the notches increases successively and corresponds to one chime.

The large wheel turns full circle once a day while the small wheel turns 20 times, running four times faster at the outside edge. The arithmetic progression is as follows:

$$1\ 2\ 3\ 4\ \underbrace{3\ 2}_{5}\ \underbrace{1\ 2\ 3}_{6}\ \underbrace{4\ 3}_{7}\ \underbrace{2\ 1\ 2\ 3}_{8}\ \underbrace{4\ 3\ 2}_{9}\ \underbrace{1\ 2\ 3\ 4}_{10}\ \underbrace{3\ 2\ 1\ 2\ 3}_{11}\ \underbrace{4\ 3\ 2\ 1\ 2}_{12}\ \cdots$$

To dramatic effect, the steps in this progression correspond to the number of chimes every hour (on the hour).

This mechanism has given rise to a mathematical model developed in honour of the clock's inventor Jan Šindel, known as the "Šindel sequence".

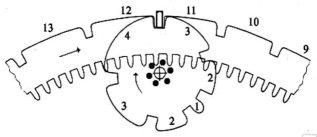

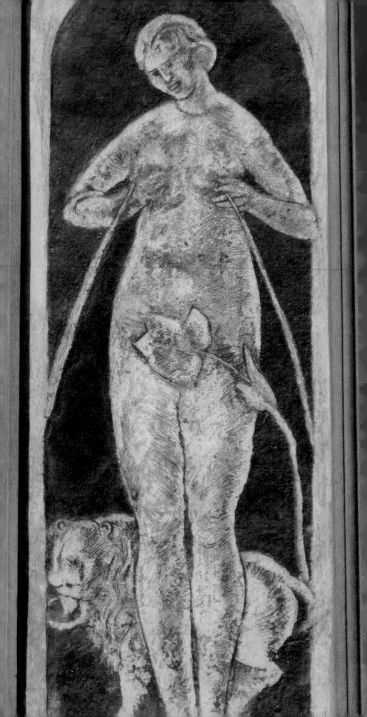

SGRAFFITO OF THE VIRGIN'S GUSHING BREAST MILK

Dům U minuty (House at the Minute)
Staroměstské náměstí (Old Town Square) 2
• Metro: Staroměstská

> *Occult allegory of the philosopher's stone?*

Near the astronomical clock in Old Town Square stands the House at the Minute. Originally a Gothic mansion, it was rebuilt twice in the Renaissance style. It has been owned by the Prague town council since the 19th century. From 1889 to 1896, the young Franz Kafka lived here with his family.

The Renaissance *sgraffito* decoration that you can admire today was only rediscovered in 1919 under a layer of old plaster.

Both façades of this house feature a set of unrelated motifs at different levels: Bacchanalia and other scenes from Graeco-Roman mythology, stories from the Old Testament (Adam and Eve, Joseph the Egyptian in the well, Jonah and the whale), depictions of the ancient Virtues and the Labours of Hercules, among many others.

Historian of hermeticism René Alleau compared this house to one of France's most important seats of alchemy, the Hôtel Lallemant at Bourges.

The last figure of the fresco on the lower east façade is a traditional allegory of Nature: a naked woman, head bowed, pressing both hands to her breasts from which two streams of liquid flow. The ancient origin of this motif is the legend of the Greek goddess Hera, who thus conceived the Milky Way.

This figure of a woman whose breasts flow with milk and blood was a very common theme in hermetic literature. One of the best known is the Virgin seated on a sperm whale in J. D. Mylius' manuscript *Philosophia reformata*, illustrating the words of Daniel Stolcius, an alchemist who studied in Prague: "The milk and blood gushing from my breasts for you – when they are boiled together – give you gold."

Another engraving, taken from *Azoth* by Basile Valentin, is of a mermaid crowned with two fishtails, swimming in the sea, with two liquids flowing from her breasts. Below this image are the lines: "I am the goddess of exceptional grandeur and beauty, born of our own sea that surrounds the moving earth. I pour the milk and blood of my breasts and cook these materials until they are converted into silver and gold."

It is understandable in this context that the *sgraffito* could evoke the Virtues of the philosopher's stone as well as the alchemist himself.

HIDDEN SYMBOLISM AT THE TWO BEARS

Kožná 1
• Metro: Můstek or Staroměstská

> *Taming the bear, an alchemical allegory*

The house known as U dvou zlatých medvědů (At the Two Bears), built between 1559 and 1567, has a beautiful Renaissance entrance with striking sculptures of two bears facing one another. Beside them are two seated men in armour proffering leafy branches.

In alchemy, the bear corresponds to the instincts and to the initial stage of the evolution of the alchemical process: it is represented by the black colour of matter in its raw or original state. It therefore appears powerful, violent, dangerous, uncontrollable, like a primitive force, and was traditionally the symbol of cruelty, savagery, brutality. However – and this higher aspect of the symbol is represented here by the men feeding the animal – the bear can also be tamed to some extent: it can dance, it can play with a ball, so it represents the alchemist's control of original matter. The bear can be tempted with honey, of which it is very fond, just as the alchemist dominates raw matter with the "honey" of wisdom. It represents, in short, the elementary forces susceptible to gradual evolution, but also to appalling aberrations such as the fake alchemists known as "windbags" who cannot back up their laboratory experiments with spiritual growth in order to achieve the highest level of alchemy – union with the divine.

Because it expresses untamed elemental matter, in Celtic society the bear was the symbol of the warrior class, and therefore of temporal power. When the bear is aggressive and cruel, it symbolizes tyranny and oppression. Tamed, it becomes the symbol of justice and freedom, reflecting the spiritual side of true alchemists – like the men depicted on the frieze at the entrance of this house, who are taming and feeding the bears.

Note also on the two side columns the hop leaves sprouting from the mouth of two recumbent heads, which might be a sign that beer (made from hops) was brewed in the house.

According to an old legend, all underground passages in Prague opened into the cellars of U dvou zlatých medvědů.

STATUE OF A PETRIFIED KNIGHT ⓲

New City Hall
Mariánské náměstí
• Metro: Staroměstská

Prague's Darth Vader

At the corner of New City Hall (Nová radnice) in Mariánské Square, the statue of a knight (sculpted by Ladislav Šaloun in the early 20th century) strangely resembles in silhouette the Darth Vader character in the George Lucas movie *Star Wars*.

The statue was erected to commemorate a legend about a demolished house at No. 119/19 Platnéřská, a street named after the armourers who had their workshops there in the 14th century.

The story goes that a knight had been seen wandering around Prague, always in black armour. As he had to have some work done on his armour, he went to Platnéřská to find a craftsman.

This man had a beautiful daughter and the stranger fell in love with her. But she refused his advances, and one day in the crowd he brutally stabbed her.

As she lay dying, the young woman cursed the knight, who was turned to stone.

Also according to legend, every hundred years, on the same day and

at the same time as the crime, the knight appears and waits for deliverance, which can only occur if an innocent girl forgives him.

He had to wait a long time until a widow and her daughter moved into this house. Exactly one hundred years after the murder, the knight appeared to the young girl. He told her not to be afraid as he was awaiting the deliverance that only she could grant him.

The girl confided her fears to her mother and, the next day, it was the mother who waited alone for the knight. At the sight of the widow, he exclaimed: "A hundred years more to wait!" and was turned back to stone.

The original house in Platnéřská Street had a sign depicting a knight called *The Iron Man,* now in Prague City Museum.

NEARBY

IDIOM – THE INFINITE COLUMN
Municipal Library of Prague
Mariánské náměstí

In the entrance hall of the Municipal Library (Městská knihovna) stands a column formed by some 8,000 books. Looking down through the opening in the centre of the column, it seems like a bottomless pit and, looking up, an endless chimney.

This feeling of infinity is the result of mirrors placed at the top and foot of the column.

The creator of this work, entitled *Idiom*, is the Slovakian artist Matej Krén.

SCULPTURE OF THE DEVIL

Žatecká 4
• Metro: Staroměstská

The Devil's in the detail

Below the central corbelling on the first floor, the façade of the early 20th-century house at No. 4 Žatecká Street features an exceptional sculpture of a horned Devil with giant bat wings, his claws gripping a coiled snake and a globe.

This unexpected apparition is somewhat offset by the colourful image of a Madonna adorned with garlands of flowers on the second floor: upstairs is dedicated to the heavenly spirits and divine powers and downstairs to the instincts, Hell and Evil.

It is interesting to note that the winged Devil is to the left of the entrance, which recalls the "Left-Hand Path" of black magic.

THE DEVIL IN PRAGUE

A vast number of Prague's legends turn on the Prince of Darkness but tangible reminders of them are few.

It is said that in the Emmaus Monastery (New Town), the Devil cooked alongside the monks.

At Prokopské údolí (Prokop valley in Prague Hlubo epy), the Devil gave no peace to St Procopius, who lived there in the city's largest cave. Over time, he managed to drive Procopius out.

At Vyšehrad, the three broken pieces of column are the result of a lost bet between the Devil and the priest (see p. 169). This legend is illustrated by the mural in the left aisle of the Church of Sts Peter & Paul.

As to the assertion that the Devil intervened in some of Prague's construction works following a pact drawn up between him and the architects, a good example is the legend of the contractor who built Charles Bridge. The story, common to many European cities, is the debt owed for his help. The assumption is that the first person to cross the new bridge will belong to the Devil.

Similarly, it is said that the architect of the vast vault of the Church of the Assumption of the Virgin Mary & Charlemagne (Karel Veliký) at Karlov (New Town) made a pact with the Devil in a moment of madness. When the vault was finished, the builders were unwilling to remove the wooden scaffolding in case the roof collapsed. The architect himself set it alight, but when the beams came crashing down in clouds of smoke and dust, he thought the vaulting had been ruined. The Devil fled and local people claimed that they had found him drowned in the waters of the Vltava later that day.

The most notorious Devil's work took place at the Faust House in Charles

Square (Karlovo nám stí). When the contract with the accursed Dr Faust expired, Mephistopheles flew in to take him to Hell. It is said that the hole in the ceiling of Faust's apartment in the south-west wing of the building took a long time to repair.

HOUSE-MUSEUM OF JAROSLAV JEŽEK

Kaprova 10, Praha 1
• Tel: 257 257 739/257 257 730 (České muzeum hudby)
• marketa_kabelkova@nm.cz
• Open Tuesday, 1pm–6pm
• Metro: Staroměstská

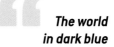

*The world
in dark blue*

I n the 1930s, the composer Jaroslav Ježek lived in a room with blue walls, ceiling and curtains. Suffering from an eye disease, he particularly appreciated this environment, which brought him a feeling of well-being. And in 1929 he wrote the song *Dark Blue World*, which describes his almost total blindness (he could only recognise shades of dark blue):

So what has happened to my eyes where is my perfect vision
Over everything spreads the impenetrable blue cloud
dark blue cloud

The room was decorated in a functionalist style by his friend, the architect František Zelenka. Among other exhibits, visitors can see the composer's original piano, his library, record collection and a few personal belongings.

JAROSLAV JEŽEK

Born in 1906 in Žižkov (Prague), Jaroslav Ježek suffered from childhood with leucoma (white opaque scar of the cornea). He attended a school for the blind in Hradčany, and was also almost deaf.

Having studied at Prague Conservatory, where he was one of the most

talented students, he teamed up with avant-garde artists such as Jiří Voskovec and Jan Werich, with whom he created an immortal trio. Ježek composed the music while Werich and Voskovec (see p. 89) wrote the lyrics. In 1934, Ježek became a member of the Surrealist group in Czechoslovakia.

After actively participating in the anti-Nazi plays of Osvobozené divadlo (Liberated Theatre or Prague Free Theatre) in January 1939 with Voskovec and Werich, he emigrated to the United States. He died there in 1942 (at the age of 35) from chronic kidney disease.

SEAT NO. 1 AT THE OLD-NEW SYNAGOGUE   ㉒
MAISELOVA

• Metro: Staroměstská; Tram: 17

Enigmas of the ghetto

Built in the second half of the 13th century during the reign of Přemysl Otakar II, the Old-New Synagogue (Staronová synagóga) is strongly associated with the extraordinary personality of the rabbi, Judah Loew ben Bezalel.

Inside, seat number 1, to the right of the cabinet where the Torah is kept, was reserved for Rabbi Loew, whose memory is still honoured by the fact that no one sits there today. Anyone presumptuous enough to do so will die within the year.

At the back wall of the synagogue, an iron staircase leads to the small door of the attic storeroom or *geniza* (see photo), to which access is forbidden. This is where Rabbi Loew is said to have kept a Golem that he deanimated by reciting a secret Kabbalistic formula.

The rabbi regularly brought the Golem back to life by placing one of the secret names of God (*shem*) in its mouth, but one day he forgot to remove the *shem* and the Golem terrorised the ghetto.

THE ANGELS OF SOLOMON'S TEMPLE IN JERUSALEM
According to legend, the synagogue was built by angels who brought stones from the destroyed Temple of Solomon, on condition that they would be returned if the temple was rebuilt in Jerusalem.
The "old-new" name of the synagogue (Staronová in Czech, *alt-neu* in German) is in fact a corruption of the Hebrew *altnai*, which means "under certain conditions". It is said that, as the ghetto was burning, two doves landed on the roof of the synagogue and by the beating of their wings saved the building from fire damage. The birds are believed to have been these angels in disguise.

WHY ARE PSALMS 92 AND 93 SUNG TWICE IN THE OLD-NEW SYNAGOGUE?

During the singing of these psalms, which marks the beginning of Shabbat (the weekly day of rest), Rabbi Loew realised his oversight. So he left the synagogue and went to extract the *shem* from the Golem.

On his return, he ordered that the two psalms should be sung again, as if nothing had happened. This explains why the two psalms are repeated in the Old-New Synagogue, a liturgical practice carried on to this day.

JUDAH LOEW BEN BEZALEL: A RABBI PASSIONATE ABOUT THE KABBALAH AND ALCHEMY?

Born in Worms according to some, in the Polish city of Pozna between 1512 and 1526 according to others, Rabbi Loew was descended from an influential rabbinical family of King David's line. He had three brothers, Chaim, Sinai and Samson, also eminent scholars. Some claim he was the youngest of the family, others that he was the oldest.

His life is surrounded by myths and legends, many of which have been popularised and are considered historical facts even if they cannot easily be verified.

Having served as rabbi in Mikulov in Moravia from 1553 to 1573, Loew went to Prague in 1573 where he founded and directed the Talmud school in the Prague ghetto. While there, he served as both judge and rabbi. He is known as the Maharal (Grand Master) of Prague and as the creator of the Golem.

On 16 February 1592, he met Emperor Rudolf II. Although the subject of their conversation is unknown, some sources claim that it was their common passion for alchemy. He also presented the emperor with a magic lantern.

His house, which stood at the junction of Široká and Pařížská streets, was later demolished along with many other houses in the Jewish quarter. The house sign is preserved in Prague City Museum.

Around 1592, Loew became Chief Rabbi at Poznań. According to contemporary reports, his frequent moves were because of his serious problems with representatives of the Prague Jewish community. However, he returned to Prague a few years later and remained there until his death in 1609, when he was buried in the Old Jewish Cemetery. Loew was recognized as a great scholar and maintained friendly contacts with Tycho Brahe and other personalities who had been attracted to Rudolf II's Prague. According to the Israeli philosopher and historian Gershom Scholem, Rabbi Loew was also devoted to the study of the Kabbalah, although he is considered the father of Hasidic Judaism whose teachings have some similarities with his own.

He left a number of written works, mainly on ethics and the interpretation of the Talmud.

THE GOLEM AND THE HEBREW KABBALAH

Whereas human beings have long dreamed of creating artificial life, the Jewish doctrine of the Kabbalah has given a homunculus the name Golem.

There is an early written account of how to create a Golem by Eleazar ben Judah of Worms (1165–1230). From the 11th century, according to tradition, the Golem had taken the form of a red clay statue (*adamaha* in Hebrew), which was endowed with life through the use of magic formulae.

Depending on the version, *emet* (truth) – one of the secret names of God – is written on the effigy's forehead or on a piece of paper inserted into its mouth to bring it to life.

According to tradition, this *shem* (short for the Hebrew term *Shemhamforash* – literally the "explicit name" [of God] among the 72 names of God) must be reset every Friday. If the word is deleted or replaced by a word for death, then the Golem returns to dust.

A Golem is traditionally a yellow Mongoloid figure, beardless and with slanting eyes.

The Golem of Prague is said to have protected the Jews from pogroms as well as working as a servant in the synagogue.

The most famous Golem was created by Rabbi Judah Loew ben Bezalel (see p. 65) in 1580, when the Jews of Prague were being accused of ritual murder and persecuted. In a prophetic dream, Rabbi Loew received the following command: "Create the Golem from clay and destroy the cities that are enemies of Israel!"(*Ata Bra Golem Hachomer Wetigzar Zedím Divuk Chewel Torfe Israel* in Hebrew.)

Note that in accordance with the Kabbalah, the words of this command begin with the first and end with the tenth letter of the Hebrew alphabet.

Tradition holds that the Golem must be made from red clay with the help of two other people, the three representing individual elements – so the rabbi (representing air) summoned his son, the priest Ben Isaac Simmson (fire) and his pupil Ben Jacob Hayyim Sasson (water). Together they went to the brickworks at the village of Košíře where, from local clay and using a ritual from the Hebrew "Book of Creation" (*Sefer Yetzira*) and a secret *shem* of Rabbi Loew, they brought the Golem to life.

There is also a tradition that one day Rabbi Loew forgot to extract the *shem*. The Golem, on the loose, terrorised the district and killed everyone it came across, forcing Rabbi Loew and his two helpers to destroy it.

The body of the Golem is allegedly kept in the attic storeroom (*geniza*) of the Old-New Synagogue. Other sources claim that it was secretly moved out to the city gates and buried in the plague cemetery (Šibeniční vrch), on the boundary of the modern districts of Vinohrady and Žižkov (see p. 199). Finally, according to legend, the Golem can reappear every 33 years.

The Hebrew word *golem* means imperfection or incompleteness – this perfectly reflects the hidden nature of the Golem of Prague, which was created as a soulless creature.

The word also appears in the Book of Psalms (16 and 139), but is usually translated as embryo, shapeless or *trupel* (old Czech).

Speculation on the creation of artificial life was also rife in hermetic writing. Paracelsus (*De generatione rerum naturalium*), for example, mentions the creation from human sperm of miniature beings known as homunculi.

CLOCK OF THE JEWISH TOWN HALL ㉓

Maiselova
• Metro: Staroměstská

Funded by the former mayor of the Jewish ghetto (Mordechai Maisel), the Jewish Town Hall (Židovská radnice) at the corner of Maiselova and Červená streets is part of the same group as the Great Synagogue built in 1577. The Rococo reconstruction of the façade dates from 1754.

A clock that runs backwards

Surprisingly, the building's clock has two dials: although one is conventional, the other is much less so as the traditional digits have been replaced by letters of the Hebrew alphabet.

In Hebrew, all the letters have a numerical value and can be used to count (based on a concept called *gematria*, the Greek word for "geometry"). Every word has a "value" obtained by totalling the numerical values of the letters.

The corresponding letters and numbers are: *aleph* (1), *beth* (2), *gimel* (3), *dalet* (4), *he* (5), *vav* (6), *zayin* (7), *het* (8), *tet* (9), *yod* (10), *yod + aleph* (11) and *yod + beth* (12). There is no single letter corresponding to 11, 12 and so on, so the appropriate letters are added together.

In addition, as Hebrew is read from right to left instead of left to right, the clock hands rotate in the opposite direction to those on a conventional clock.

The Hebrew clock was designed in 1764 by Šebestián Landesberger, royal clockmaker at the Prague court.

STAR OF DAVID, A SYMBOL FIRST ASSOCIATED WITH THE PRAGUE JEWS
The identification of Judaism with the Star of David began in the Middle Ages: it first came about in 1354, when Charles IV bestowed on Prague's Jewish community the privilege of having its own flag. So the Jews designed a hexagram or six-pointed star of gold on a red background, which was known as the Shield of David (Magen David in Hebrew) and became an official symbol of the synagogues and the Jewish community in general. In the 19th century, this symbol appeared everywhere.

For more on the Star of David and its mystic symbolism, see p. 150.

BAS-RELIEF OF A MAN WITH A MOUSTACHE 24

Vltava embankment below the Convent of the Knights of the Cross
• Metro: Staroměstská; Tram: 17

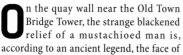

On the quay wall near the Old Town Bridge Tower, the strange blackened relief of a mustachioed man is, according to an ancient legend, the face of the first builder of Judith Bridge, precursor of Charles Bridge. This head was originally set in the last arch of Judith Bridge, near the pillar.

A medieval stream gauge

Local people call him Bradáč (the bearded man) because of his hirsuteness.

Thanks to its stable site, this sculpture has frequently served as a stream gauge, using different parts of the face to measure the height of the Vltava waters and the associated flood risk.

Thus when the water reached the lower parts of Bradáč's beard, this meant that the Vltava would soon overflow and people in low-lying areas along the banks moved out.

If the water began to reach his mouth, the river would flood the streets on the Old Town side.

Finally, if the water covered his head completely, the only way to reach Old Town Square was by boat.

The sandstone sculpture was mentioned for the first time in 1432 in the Old Czech Almanac.

OTHER ANCIENT FLOOD MARKERS IN PRAGUE

The oldest Prague flood markers are at the Convent of the Knights of the Cross with the Red Star (Křižovnický klášter) in the Old Town (floods in 1675 and 1890). Nearby is another Bradáč, used since the 15th century as a stream gauge.

House No. 514 on the Kampa island side of the Vltava, in Malá Strana: commemorative metal and stone plaques (floods of 1784, 1845 and 1890).

Embankment about 5 metres above Most Legií (Bridge of Legions) in Malá Strana: flood markers from 1784, 1845, 1862, 1872 and 1876.

Clam-Gallas Palace, No. 158/20 Husova Street in the Old Town: flooding in March and October 1845.

Pillars of the railway viaduct, Podbabská Street, Prague 6: floods of 1876, 1890 and 1896.

VĚŽNÍK STATUE

Staroměstská věž Karlova mostu
• October–March, daily 10am–8pm
November–February, daily 10am–6pm
April–September, daily 10am–10pm
• Metro: Staroměstská; Tram: 17, 18, Karlovy lázně stop

The Quasimodo of Prague

Concealed at the top of the steps of the Old Town Bridge Tower, on the Old Town side, the statue of Věžník (the guardian of the tower) is probably the most remarkable sculpture in Prague.

It represents an old man with a large hump, which has earned him the nickname, the "Quasimodo of Prague". The sandstone is worn away but the bending hunchback can be seen lifting his tunic to expose his right leg. At his belt hangs a sheathed knife.

In the opinion of some historians, this could be King Wenceslas IV's humorous reaction to the solemnity of the symbolic statues erected on the orders of his father (Charles IV) on this same tower. Remember that the statue could originally be seen by everybody: it gazed down with its majestic features on the coronation procession. It was only when the tower was renovated in the late 19th century that the statue was hidden under the roof.

Another explanation for this statue has been provided by the French hermetic historian René Alleau: he found that the characteristic gesture of the leg with knee uncovered is the occult symbol of the "Brotherhood of Fools" founded at Cleves in 1380.

According to Alleau, this symbol therefore indicates "the hermetic wisdom hidden under an apparent madness, based on the study of two worlds, the heavenly and the earthly, their union having the knee as an emblem".

The hunchback guardian – probably also a reference to Atlas, who supported the pillars that held Heaven and Earth – not only symbolizes the union of the two worlds, but also the possibility of their division, which is represented by the knife. This is one of the most authentic records of medieval esotericism in the Czech Republic.

SECRETS OF CHARLES BRIDGE

Charles Bridge Museum, Křížovnické náměstí 3
• Metro: Staroměstská; Tram 12, 17 or 22

> ## *Charles Bridge: link to the Royal Way*

In Charles Bridge, the number of arches, the relationship between them, and the total length and orientation are by no means coincidental.

Thus the bridge heads east to west, following its overall conception, in the direction of the Royal Way and its significance, which is both exoteric and esoteric (see p. 16).

Charles Bridge is 515 metres long: this is also the distance between the 44 small chapels lining the route from Prague to Stará Boleslav, where St Wenceslas was murdered. It was moreover via this bridge that the relics of St Wenceslas were transferred from Stará Boleslav to Prague Castle on 4 March 932 (or 938 according to some sources).

While initially the bridge had no ornamentation, crosses were quickly installed under the rule of Charles IV, since when they have been replaced several times.

Later, a Hebrew inscription praising God was affixed under a Christ on the Cross. According to legend, this was ordered by the Royal Court in 1696 following the conviction of a Jew who had violated the Cross.

In the 17th century 30 statues, mainly Baroque in style, were erected one by one on the parapets of the bridge. They form an extraordinary gallery of saints associated with many legends. Note that they are almost all gazing westwards towards the Royal Way and its esoteric goal – the spiritual work that will sanctify us all on the road to philosophical gold and spiritual enlightenment.

On the orders of King Wenceslas IV, John of Nepomuk (Jan Nepomucký), later canonised, was thrown from Charles Bridge for refusing to divulge the confessional secrets of Queen Sophia. It is said that the bridge pier at the point where the priest was thrown into the river then collapsed, an incident generally considered as the work of the Devil. Legend also says that the master mason contracted to restore the bridge made a pact with the Devil, promising him the soul of the first person who crossed over. That person was none other than his own wife.

One of the bridge pillars is also supposed to conceal a treasure, hidden there by Templar monks during the suppression of their Order. It is said to contain a mason's hammer used in the construction of the Tower of Babel, as well as a large rock crystal from King Solomon's crown. The treasure will be found, it is said, when the reign of Christ on Earth begins.

PALINDROME OF CHARLES BRIDGE: 135797531

The timing of the construction of Charles Bridge is extraordinary: after consultation with the mathematician Havel of Strahov to determine the best time to lay the first stone, Charles IV chose the date 9 July 1357 (Julian calendar), at 5.31 in the morning. This timing made it possible to set up a rather remarkable numerical palindrome:

1357, **9** July (the **7**th month), to **5** hours **31** minutes in the morning gives the number **135797531**, which could be read in both directions and also all prime numbers (non-divisible) to a single digit, in addition to the 9.

The sum of the digits of the year of construction (1 + 3 +5 +7 +9) is the same as the number of arches in the bridge (25).

Interestingly, a textual palindrome was supposedly discovered on the Old Town Bridge Tower. It is believed that this used a so-called "magic trap" like the one on the tower of New Town Hall (Novoměstská radnice) – see p. 96.

CHARLES BRIDGE AND ASTROLOGY

On the date of the bridge's foundation – 9 July 1357 – all the planets known at the time, with the exception of Mars, were in the most favourable astrological position above the horizon (Mars is a symbol of great achievements, but also of war).

Mars and the Moon were also in the signs of Cancer and Pisces, and so were in the water signs of the zodiac, an aspect obviously favourable for building a bridge over a river.

Finally, the Sun was in the sign of Leo, the heraldic symbol of the Czech kingdom, and Saturn was in conjunction with the Sun, considered a good omen at the time as the negative influence of Saturn would be overcome by the positive action of the Sun.

SYMBOLISM OF THE STATUE OF ST CHRISTOPHER

Charles Bridge
• Metro: Staroměstská

> **St Christopher carrying Christ and the alchemical gold**

Although Charles Bridge is the route of the alleged Royal Way to the castle and the coronation procession of a new king, it is also the route to the alchemical process leading to the manufacture of the philosopher's stone (see p. 16).

Almost in the middle of the bridge, the sixth pillar on the left was a sentry box. There is now a statue of St Christopher, the work of sculptor E. Max, which was erected in the mid-19th century. This is the only statue heading westwards on Charles Bridge.

In the occult topography of Prague's Royal Way, "young gold" (in the alchemical sense) was born on the right bank of the Vltava River (to the east), in the centre of the Old Town, and it needed a porter who could transport the "boy king" (Jesus, i.e. the alchemical gold) to the other side of the river.

Although the statue of St Christopher was the last to be placed on Charles Bridge, it is still within the esoteric concept of the Royal Way and shows that the siting of relatively recent artefacts may unconsciously reflect the precise hermetic meaning of their surroundings, and thus fit in with the all-powerful spirit of a place (*genius loci*).

LEGEND OF ST CHRISTOPHER, BEARER OF CHRIST

In the story of Christopher as transcribed by Jacob of Voragine in his *Golden Legend*, Offerus, a pagan giant, decided to serve the greatest king of the country. Caught in the clutches of the Devil, the king freed himself by making the sign of the Cross, upon which Offerus concluded that the king was more powerful than the Devil. One day as Offerus was helping travellers to cross the river, he met the young Christ, who baptised him and named him Christopher or "bearer of Christ" (*Christo-foros*, in Greek). This legend has long been cited, notably in hermeticism, because of the homophony of the name Christos with the Greek word *chrysos*, meaning gold. St Christopher is synonymous with the bearer of gold (*Chrysophoros*) to alchemists.

NOVÉ MĚSTO

"NEW ROCOCO" INTERIOR OF THE POSTAL MUSEUM ❶

Novomlýnská 2
- Tel: 222 312 006
- Open every day except Monday, 9am–12 noon and 1pm–5pm
- Tram: 5, 8, 14, 26, Dlouhá třída stop

Philately in a former mill

With its rich collections of Czech and foreign stamps, the Postal Museum (Poštovní muzeum) is located in Prague's only surviving old mill – it escaped demolition thanks to its extraordinary "new Rococo" interior.

The building, which is also known as the Vávra mill (Vávrův mlýn), was rebuilt in Baroque and classical style on foundations dating back to the Renaissance. The beautiful frescoes are the main attraction of its typical Biedermeier-period* interior: it was in 1847 that the miller V. Michalovic asked his friend, the renowned Czech painter Josef Navrátil, to undertake the interior design.

Today you can visit the dining room where there is a huge still life with a lobster, and several other remarkably decorated rooms featuring alpine landscapes and well-known characters from plays and operas of the time. In the living room, the original tiled stove was also built to Navrátil's design.

*A trend in central Europe for artistic styles named after "Papa Biedermeier", a comic symbol parodying petit-bourgeois family life and activities.

SYMBOLISM "AT THE GOLDEN SUN"

Na Poříčí 22
• Tram: 3, 8, 24, Bílá labuť stop

> **On the road with St Wenceslas ...**

Rebuilt in the early 19th century in classical style, the house known as "At the Golden Sun" owes its name to two suns that feature on the triangular pediment and above the door.

They remind us that we are on the route taken by the body of St Wenceslas (Václav) at his funeral. This path leading to Prague from Stará Boleslav, east of the capital, was an important pilgrimage site.

The Czech king and duke of Bohemia, St Wenceslas (born around 907 and died in 927 or 935) is the patron saint of Bohemia.

In the context of Czech mythology he was associated with the Sun for its classic attributes of strength, power and authority, but also because, just as the Sun gives life, Wenceslas gave birth to the Czech nation.

LEGIOBANKA BUILDING

Na Poříčí 24
• Tram: 3, 8, 24, Bila labuť stop

> *A Czech architectural speciality: Rondocubism*

The Bank of Czechoslovak Legions (Legiobanka) is a spectacular example of the Czech style known as Rondocubism (and sometimes National Style or "rotund Cubism"): the original Cubist right-angles, cubes and pyramids have been rounded out in the spirit of Slavic tradition. When the style first emerged, it attracted harsh criticism from architectural pundits.

The building was commissioned for the bank founded in 1919 to aid Czechoslovak legionnaires in Russia and France (so they could deposit their surplus earnings). It was designed by architect Josef Gočár and his artist friends Jan Štursa (responsible for the four sculptures of legionnaires on top of the main entrance pillars), Otto Gutfreund (who created the sandstone relief on the second-floor balcony with battle scenes and the returning legions) and

František Kysela, designer of the stained-glass window in the form of a three-leaved flower above the entrance hall. Kysela also carried out the decorative paintings inside the bank. The original design has been perfectly preserved in the first-floor waiting rooms.

The bank's furnishings were also made to the sketches of Josef Gočár.

After the Second World War, Legiobanka was nationalised and merged with the Czechoslovak Bank of Commerce. The building was enlarged in 1991.

Prague's famous first cabaret, U Bucků (along with a beer of the same name) could be found in the mid-19th-century house demolished in the 1930s to make way for Legiobanka.

POWER PLANT TURBINE ❹

Štvanice island
• Metro: Vltavská; Tram: 1, 3, 5, 25, Vltavská stop

A discreet industrial relic

At the tip of the largest point of Štvanice island, an ostensibly strange object rests on a concrete base.

The Art Nouveau hydraulic electricity plant built on the island in 1913 was renovated in the 1980s. At the same time, more powerful turbines were installed and one of the old turbines was moved to the southern tip of the island as a souvenir.

This plant was one of the first concrete constructions in Prague.

SYMBOLISM "AT THE GOLDEN SHIP"

⑤

Zlatnická 7
• Tram: 3, 5, 14, 24, 26, Masarykovo nádraží stop

A curious navigational aid

It's easy to overlook the semicircular pediment on top of the house called U zlaté lodi (At the Golden Ship), which shows a sailor wearing a hat in a ship loaded with an anchor and a small barrel.

To the left of the pediment is a statue of a helmeted Mercury carrying a caduceus, winged sandals on his feet, while to the right Fortuna is represented bearing a cornucopia.

If at first glance the scene is an allegory and a celebration of the nascent bourgeoisie, careful consideration (given the context of the city – see p. 16) of the orientation of the gable in the topography of Prague, the path of the ship sailing from left to right and the marine pilot who sets his course to the north, where the North Star lies, suggests that another meaning may be hidden here.

The alchemists often concealed their subject in the form of a ship, also referred to as a vessel, which can mean container or apparatus.

To navigate by the North Star (Cynosura or Polaris) was the goal of all alchemists, to prevent the ship from venturing into the perilous northern

waters and being wrecked (*Naufragio philosophorum*).

The region around the pole was, according to legend, inhabited by the remora, an extraordinary fish of the Echeneidae family which is said to have the power to calm storms and quell the waves.

For alchemists, this fish, sometimes depicted as a dolphin, was the agent of Mercury that aided them in their voyages. To them it was an experienced navigator, the first and vital sign in the troubled sea, *Le Pilote de l'onde vive* (Pilot of the Living Wave) in the words of Mathurin Eyquem du Martineau, author of a book of that name.

The anchor is an ancient symbol of hope, which can bring ships to a halt; and when the heraldic dolphin is curled around it, it can calm the storm, just like the remora.

The two statues that feature with this maritime scene also refer to philosophical navigation: Mercury, the protector of travellers but also the legendary founder of alchemy, from whose Greek name Hermes the word hermeticism is derived; and Fortuna, goddess of chance and luck, symbol of future achievement, whose attributes are the wheel, sphere, rudder, ship's bow (heading towards her on the pediment) and the cornucopia she holds in her arms.

The Flowers of Heaven spilling from the cornucopia represent the materialisation of the spirit of base metals and indicate that the owner of this house was particularly advanced in his alchemical work.

PATERNOSTER ELEVATOR

YMCA Palace - Na Poříčí 12
• Tram: 3, 8, 24, Bílá labuť stop

> ### *Over the top ...*

The YMCA Palace, built in 1928 by the architect E. Hnilička, has one of Prague's best-preserved examples of a "paternoster" elevator.

The principle of these rather distinctive machines is simple: no doors, no stops, you just take the elevator "on the fly" ... right cabin to go up, left to go down. Your first reaction, in theory, is positive: no need to wait for long minutes wondering what's going on a few floors above. In practice, the system can be rather confusing. Although it moves rather slowly, which is obviously better, some people find it disconcerting. It's true though that you should still step in smartly when a cabin passes, otherwise you'll be left behind.

But there's no denying that after the first surprise, it all runs smoothly.

When visiting the building, ask the caretaker to kindly let you try out the elevator.

WHY "PATERNOSTER"?

The name of this legendary elevator comes from the loop system: the movement of cabins suspended from two chains driven by gears evokes the rosary beads used as an aid when reciting the Lord's Prayer (*paternoster* being Latin for "Our Father").

A paternoster elevator consists of a set of cabins suspended one above the other, held in place by chains which rotate without interruption and in which passengers step on or off without the elevator stopping. Once at the top of the chain, each cabin descends to the foot of the shaft only to rise again, in endless slow motion.

The system was invented in 1877 by Frederick Hart (the first paternoster was installed in the English county of Kent) – it has spread throughout Europe and is especially popular in Eastern Europe.

Its success was originally due to the fact that it carries more people per unit of time than conventional elevators and, at 15 cm/second, is faster than an escalator.

Nowadays, these elevators are tending to disappear, both because of the greater risk of accidents (five people were killed between 1970 and 1993 and an 81-year-old man died in 2012 when he fell into the shaft) and because their speed is limited by definition (passengers need time to get on and off). Also, classic elevators are now highly efficient: the cars of the Mitsubishi elevator in Yokohama travel at 45 km/hour (over nine times the speed of a paternoster).

PRAGUE PATERNOSTERS OPEN TO THE PUBLIC:

The first paternoster was installed in 1911 in the new Prague City Hall. Currently, the oldest paternoster elevator still in service is in the Czech Radio building in Vinohrady. Of the 110 "up-and-over" elevators in the Czech Republic, some 70 are still working. These are accessible to the public:

YMCA Palace, Na Poříčí 12, Praha 1
Dopravní podniky building, Bubenská 1, Praha 7
Lucerna Palace, Štěpánská 61, Praha 1
U Novaku Palace, Vodičkova 28, 30, V Jámě 1, 3, 5, Praha 1
Petzek Palace, Politických vězňů 20, Praha 1
Praha 7 Municipal House, Captain Jaroš embankment 1000/7, Praha 7
Družstevní asociace house, Těšnov 5, Praha 1
Faculty of Law, Curieových náměstí 7, Praha 1
Praha 1 Municipal House, Vodičkova 18, Praha 1
Revenue Offices, Štěpánská 28, Praha 1
Dunaj Palace, Národni 10, Praha 1
Prague City Hall, Mariánske náměstí 2, Praha 1
Škoda Palace, Jungmannova 35, Praha 1

OSVOBOZENÉ
DIVADLO

VOSKOVEC
& WERICH

← DENNĚ

PO DIVADLE KONCERT

V GRANDKAVÁRNE

←

MURAL ADVERTISEMENT FOR V + W   ❼

U Nováků building
V Jámě

*Souvenir
of the Liberated
Theatre*

The façade of the U Nováků building on V Jámě Street is covered with a remarkable original advertisement for the actors Jiří Voskovec and Jan Werich and their company, Osvobozené divadlo. The mural is attributed to F. Zelinka, the theatre's set designer.

LIBERATED THEATRE AND V + W

In late 1925, the Devětsil association of artists and architects founded the avant-garde troupe Osvobozené divadlo (Liberated Theatre or Prague Free Theatre), as Jiří Frejka dubbed it.

Influenced by Dadaism, Futurism and Poetism and strongly left-wing, this group – led by Frejka, Jindřich Honzl and Emil František Burian – targeted bourgeois society.

During its lifetime the group presented the works of Apollinaire, Jarry, Cocteau, Breton, Marinetti and Nezval.

When the theatre moved into U Nováků in 1930, the two actors Voskovec and Werlich (V + W) joined the group. They were soon collaborating with Jaroslav Ježek, who wrote the music for their scripts, and Honzl, an avant-garde filmmaker who produced their shows.

Until 1932, their scripts criticised the social conditions of Czechoslovakia and the rest of the world. The V + W duo were the stars of the show, with masks modelled on the Fratellini brothers and humour inspired by Charlie Chaplin.

Shortly before the Second World War, the two got into deep water

over censorship and were finally obliged to emigrate to the United States.

They are particularly well known for their "Forbina" show (from the German *Vorbühne*, meaning "in the foreground"), with improvised dialogue dealing with political and cultural news.

The Liberated Theatre did not carry on after the war.

FROG AT U NOVÁKŮ

8

Vodičkova 28
V Jámě 1, 3, 5
• Metro: Můstek; Tram: 3, 9, 14, 24, Václavské náměstí stop

Legend
of the Frog King

Built between 1901 and 1904 by the architect Oskar Polívka, the Art Nouveau U Nováků building is garlanded with remarkable plant forms and superb mosaics designed by Symbolist painter Jan Preisler.

Below the second-floor windows, note the statues of two amphibians. Their golden crowns and red linen scarves are a reference to the old Slavic legend of the Frog King.

This recounts that the magic crown can be captured when the frog has laid it down on a red linen scarf before jumping into the water. Provided a thief does not look back, he can steal the crown without danger.

A similar legend tells the story of the crown of the Snake King, which is illustrated below the first-floor windows.

In the basement is the ABC theatre where the Osvobozené divadlo company played in the 1930s with its famous actors Jiří Voskovec and Jan Werich (see preceding page).

THE CUBIST AUREOLE ON THE STATUE ❾
OF JOHN NEPOMUK

Near the Church of the Holy Trinity, Spálená
• Metro: Národní třída; Tram: 3, 9, 14, 22, 24, Lazarská stop

*A Cubist
saint*

Between the Baroque Church of the Holy Trinity (Nejsvětější Trojice) and the Diamond villa (pre-Cubist), the statue of John Nepomuk by Baroque sculptor M. V. Jäckel is surrounded by a wonderful Cubist aureole designed by A. Pfeiffer in 1913.

The Church of the Holy Trinity – built in 1713 by architect O. Broggio – originally belonged to the Holy Trinity Monastery. It is now the Prague seat of the Slovak Catholics.

Built between 1912 and 1913 in pre-Cubist style by architects E. Blecha and E. Králíček on the site of the former monastery at the junction of Spálená and Lazarská streets, the Diamond villa takes its name from its Cubist décor, which is preserved almost in its entirety both inside and outside.

The five points on the small copper roof over the statue recall the five stars around the saint's head (see p. 131).

INSIGNIA AT U BISKUPSKÉ ČEPICE PALACE 🔟

Opatovická 20
• Metro: Národní třída; Tram: 3, 9, 14, 24, Lazarská stop; tram14,
Myslikova stop

> *Symbols
> of a secret Masonic
> order, according
> to Meyrink?*

Above the main entrance to the palace that once belonged to the abbot of a Prague monastery, at the corner of Opatovická Street, is an escutcheon depicting a unicorn and a boar's head with a mitre set over them. This insignia expresses the balance between animality, virility and the forces of evil, represented by the boar's head; and humility, virginity and purity, symbolised by the unicorn.

Gustav Meyrink, in some of his stories, attaches great significance to this palace and its insignia. In *Invisible Prague*, he says: "When I arrived in Opatovická Street, above the door of a respectable patrician's house I saw a sign carved in stone that had been a feature of the Sath-Bhai – Asiatic Brethren – and was surmounted by a mitre."

In the story *The White Parrot of Dr Haselmayer* he again evokes the palace and its sign: "The stone insignia on the wall, above the entrance gate, in one's line of vision, shows the symbols and signs of the ancient Asiatic order of the Sath-Bhai, written about in books lost for centuries: the boar, seven birds with crossed beaks, etc. The mitre, later placed over the sign, conceals the secret of its origins."

Meyrink thus revives an old Masonic legend relating to the secret order of Sath-Bhai, the Asiatic Brethren. According to this legend, seven monks of this order from Allahabad (India) had established seats there known as *prah* ("threshold" in ancient Sanskrit). The monks having also settled in Bohemia, the Sanskrit word *prah* gave rise to the name the city of Prague (Praha in Czech), a place of transition between the visible world and the invisible one.

Invisible Prague by Gustav Meyrink is a poetic vision due partly to his conversion to Buddhism towards the end of his life: the insignia

he describes is in fact that of the Monastery of Svatý Jan pod Skalou (St John under the Cliff), near the Bohemian town of Beroun. Bearing the inscription AASJ (Aedes Abbatis Sancti Joannis – St John's Abbey), it dates from 1719 and probably represents the arms of Abbot Koterovsky (1695–1742) who rebuilt this palace.

GUSTAV MEYRINK

Gustav Meyrink, the pen-name of Gustav Meyer (1868–1932), was a German-language writer who drew inspiration from the ambiance of Prague's Old Town, mainly the Jewish ghetto.

Born in Vienna, he lived in Prague from 1884 where he set up a bank with money inherited from his father, while frequently meeting up with the German and Czech neo-romantics of the time.

Meyrink was a troubled man who had difficulty getting over the tragic suicide of his son, Harro Fortunat, and was constantly trying to escape from poverty when his literary efforts found little success.

During his time in Prague, at the end of his tether, Meyrink was considering suicide. But, just as he was loading his Spanish revolver, a pamphlet about life after death was slipped under the door. He put off his suicide attempt, leafing through the occult literature to which he was so attracted.

In 1891, he became the co-founder and president of an esoteric lodge, "At the Blue Star", to which mystical figures such as Prague's Karel Weinfürter and the writers Julius Zeyer and Emanuel Lešehrad also belonged. The lodge met in his apartment at No. 10 Národní třída in the Schwerts-Wallis villa, where he lived until 1929.

He was also interested in Eastern sciences, the occult and the history of sects, orders and secret societies.

In 1904, victimised by hostile neighbours and police harassment following false allegations of bank fraud, as well as animosity to his sardonic stories and antimilitarism, he decided to leave Prague for good.

After some time in Vienna, Munich and Montreux, he spent the rest of his life in the Bavarian town of Starnberg.

His short stories and tales reflecting his admiration for Old Prague include *The Golem*, *The White Dominican*, *Walpurgis Night*, *The Green Face* and *The Angel of the West Window*.

ETALON

(BÝVALÁ ÚŘEDNÍ MÍRA)
PRAŽSKÉHO LOKTE ZVANÉHO TEŽ ČEŠSKÝ,
JENŽ BYL STANOVEN ZA KRÁLE PŘEMYSLA
OTAKARA II. V ROCE 1268, ...
ZDE SI MOHLI KUPCI ČEŠÍ ...
I DŘÍVE CIMENTOVAT SVÉ DŘEVĚNÉ LOKTE.
BYL ZDE ZAZDĚN, PROTOŽE KAŽDÝ
MÁ JE K TOMU PŘÍSTUP VOLNÝ, I MĚL OU
MÍRU TOHOLOKTE PRAŽŠKEHO SOBĚ
VZÍTI MOHL.

PRAGUE STANDARD CUBIT

Nové Město Town Hall
Karlovo náměstí (Charles Square) 23
Vodičkova 1
• Metro: Karlovo náměstí; Tram: 3, 6, 18, 21, 22, 24, Karlovo náměstí stop

O n the wall of the New Town Hall in Vodičková Street, a metal bar is fixed in a vertical position.

The unit of measurement until 1765

As explained on the plaque below, this etalon (standard) is a cubit (591.4 millimetres) typically used in Prague to make accurate measurements of goods for sale and thus avoid disputes.

The Prague cubit, introduced as a unit of measurement by King Přemysl Otakar II in 1268, was used until January 1765 when Empress Maria Theresa ordered the use of the Viennese standard cubit, as in her native Lower Austria.

HOW IS A METRE DEFINED?

It is all too often forgotten that the metre is a French invention, defined by the Paris Académie des Sciences in 1791 as one ten millionth of a quarter of a meridian of the earth. By this definition, the circumference (that is, meridian) of the Earth was 40,000km. After the establishment of the first standard metre, it was 1875 before seventeen other nations signed the "Convention du Mètre". In 1899, the Bureau of Weights and Measures had a standard metre cast in platinum-iridium alloy, which was held to be subject to only infinitesimal variations; that original bar can still be seen at the Pavillon de Breteuil in Sèvres (France). With the advent of laser technology, the Conférence Générale des Poids et Mesures (CGPM) in 1960 gave a definition of the metre that is rather less comprehensible to the layman: 1,650,763.73 wavelengths of orange-coloured radiation emitted by the krypton 86 atom.

In 1983 came an even more esoteric definition: the metre is the length of the path travelled by light in vacuum during a time interval of 1/299,792,458 of a second. According to the theory of relativity, the speed of light in vacuum is the same at all points, so this definition is considered to be more accurate.

TOWN HALL PALINDROME

Nové Město Town Hall
Karlovo náměstí (Charles Square) 23 - Vodičkova 1
• Metro: Karlovo náměstí; Tram: 3, 6, 18, 21, 22, 24, Karlovo náměstí stop

Warding off the Devil

In the centre of the south wall of the New Town Hall (about 2.5 metres above the ground), two now almost illegible lines are inscribed:

"SIGNATESIGNATEMEREMETANGISETANGIS
ROMATIBISUBITOMOTIBUSIBITAMOR"
WENCESLAVS I

(Appearing as a constellation [of the sky], Rome, you touch me and desire me in vain,

But by the movements [of the stars], love will suddenly come to you)

This is a remarkably impressive double palindrome in which both lines can be read either backwards or forwards: this is thought to have been intended to defend the Town Hall from the Devil.

There is another, perhaps more realistic, interpretation wherein the inscription relates to the executions that used to be held outside the Town Hall.

On most occasions, the condemned man was allowed to say a prayer and kiss the Cross. This would explain the lines translated as: "You cross yourself, you cross yourself in vain, you touch me, from Rome help will quickly come to you."

There is a similar inscription on the Old Town Bridge Tower, for the same reasons (see p. 75).

NEARBY

CHAIN ON THE TOWN HALL DOOR

Not far from the standard cubit, a chain is anchored in the wall. This is a vestige of the system used to close off Vodičkova Street (like other streets in medieval Prague) to separate the Town Hall from the rest of the square.

ALCHEMICAL FRESCOES OF FAUST HOUSE ⑭

Karlovo náměstí (Charles Square) 40
• Metro: Karlovo náměstí; Tram: 3, 6, 18, 21, 22, 24, Karlovo náměstí or
Moráň stop

*House
of mystery*

O n the ground floor of the corner tower of Faust House (see below), which now belongs to Charles University, there are Renaissance frescoes depicting alchemical artefacts (crucible and mortar). This is probably the part of the house that was used for alchemical experiments.

In the early 15th century, it was well known that the Princes of Opava carried out alchemy experiments in their palace, probably built in the late 13th century on the site of the present house.

In 1590, Edward Kelley, an English charlatan who was for a while alchemist at the court of Emperor Rudolf II, took over the house, and in 1721 Ferdinand Antonín Mladota of Solopysky practised chemistry there. His son Joseph, an expert in mechanics, continued his work. The Mladota family manufactured and sold a so-called miraculous preparation obtained from Hradčany shale. Visitors to the house at the time were impressed by moving figurines and staircases, not to mention mysterious sounds seeming to come from nowhere.

Dr Karl Jaenig, curate of the neighbouring Church of St John on the Rock (Jana Nepomuckého na Skalce), who lived there in the early 20th century, probably fuelled the legends surrounding this house. Rumour has it that he collected objects connected with death and the gallows and slept in a coffin.

THE HOLE WHERE MEPHISTOPHELES WHISKED FAUST OFF TO HELL?
According to legend, the house at No. 40 Charles Square was one of the residences of the notorious Dr Faust (see following page).
On the ceiling plaster of the second-floor bedroom in the corner tower, inexplicable stigmata (a hole and stains) led people to think that, after the expiry of the pact between Faust and the Devil, Mephistopheles dragged him off to Hell through the roof.
Surprisingly, during the Anglo-American air raid of 14 February 1945, a bomb fell through the house in exactly the same place but from roof to cellar, without exploding. The seven cats long ago walled up alive in the house were thought to have protected it from complete destruction. Their skeletons were actually found within the walls. After the Second World War, the house was completely restored so there is no longer any trace of the former damage.

Another legend says that secret underground passages lead from Faust House to the Town Hall on the opposite side of Charles Square.

THE REAL DOCTOR JOHANNES FAUST

Made famous by Goethe who dramatised the Faust story in two of his plays, Dr Faust is the hero of the chapbook *Historia von D. Johann Fausten* published by Johann Spies in 1587. In this collection of tales, Faust is a scholar disappointed by his research who makes a pact with the Devil in the shape of the fiend Mephistopheles, who offers him another life of material pleasures, all for the price of his soul.

Other texts, such as the manuals of magic spells *Höllenzwang* and *Magia naturalis et innaturalis*, published in Passau (Bavaria) in the 16th century, describe the workings and rituals of black magic falsely attributed to Faust. In the early 17th century, English actors spread the Faust legend throughout Bohemia, embellished with elements from the similar legend of Žito, a former magician, who had lived at the court of Wenceslas IV in the early 15th century.

It seems that all these texts were inspired by an actual person, even though the realism of the character varies according to the source.

According to the most common of these, the real Dr Johannes (or Georgius) Faust was born around 1480. In the early 16th century, he is thought to have been a professional teacher at Kreuznach on the Rhine (central Germany), then moved to Erfurt and Bamberg where he cast horoscopes at the request of the bishop. His black magic practices led to him being banished from Ingolstadt in 1528 and Nuremberg in 1532. He is said to have died around 1536.

According to other sources, the real Faust lived in the guise of a certain Dr Sabellicus Georgius, Faustus junior, whom it was said studied supernatural

magic at the University of Kraków in Poland and was accused of practising black magic.

Finally, for some people, Faust was none other than Johann Fust of Mainz, one of the inventors of printing, whose life was scarred by these scurrilous tales.

Because of Faust's extraordinary personality, a legend began to develop around his life, claiming that he had a pact with the Devil.

COLOURFUL TANK AT THE POLICE MUSEUM

Ke Karlovu 453/1, Praha 2
• Tel: 974 824 855
• www.muzeumpolicie.cz
• Open Tuesday to Sunday, 10am to 5pm

> *The extraordinary story of a villager who tried to flee in a tank*

The small tank in the garden behind the Police Museum at Karlov was built in 1969–70 by Vladimír Beneš, a villager from Hrušky, near the town of Břeclav in Moravia. With his wife and children, he used it to try and cross the border between Communist Czechoslovakia and Austria on the night of 19 May 1970. The tank's gun was intended to break through the barbed wire at the border.

Unluckily not everything went as planned – the tank broke down almost at the border and Beneš abandoned it there, eventually crossing on foot and leaving his family in Czechoslovakia. He fled to the United States.

It was not until seven years later that he obtained a travel permit for his family, thanks to the intervention of the Red Cross, so that they could join him.

ylobates)

HRDLIČKA MUSEUM OF ANTHROPOLOGY   ⑯

Viničná 7
• Open every Wednesday and Friday, 10am–6pm
• Metro: I. P. Pavlova; Tram: 4, 6, 10, 16, 22, I. P. Pavlova stop; Bus: 291, Větrov stop

> *A real cabinet of curiosities*

Officially opened on 22 October 1937, the Hrdlička Museum of Anthropology is a wonderful institution open to the public two days a week. The museum is named after Aleš Hrdlička (1869–1943), a Czech anthropologist who emigrated with his family to the United States, where he spent most of his life.

Hrdlička is best known for formulating the hypothesis of human migration from Asia to North America across the Bering Strait (which separates Siberia from Alaska).

This small museum (only two rooms), founded thanks to the donation of Hrdlička's personal collection, crams many rare objects into a small space. Exhibits include the death masks of Czech presidents, Egyptian mummies, comparative skeletons of primates and humans, anatomical casts, maps, and much more.

Charles University Faculty of Science, in the same premises as the museum, was the headquarters of the Institute of Theoretical Physics in 1911. A commemorative plaque recalls that Albert Einstein was a professor there in 1911–12.

CANNONBALLS AT ST CHARLEMAGNE'S

Karlov
• Bus: 291, Dětská nemocnice Karlov stop

> *Souvenir*
> *of the 1757 battle*

Black marks that can be seen on the wall of the Church of the Assumption of the Virgin Mary & Charlemagne (sv Karel Veliký) are the remains of 11 cannonballs fired by the Prussians from the other side of the Nusle valley, near what is now Vyšehrad metro station.

During the Seven Years' War (1756–63), the Prussian troops led by Emperor Frederick II entered Bohemia and fought several bloody battles with the Austrian troops. In 1757, after the battle of Šterboholy, the Prussian army besieged Prague. The Prussians bombarded Karlov and demolished the church towers but the dome remained intact.

Karlov hill is an oasis of tranquillity in the city centre.

The church dedicated to Karel Veliký was built by Emperor Charles IV

along similar lines to the funerary chapel of Charlemagne at Aix-la-Chapelle (Aachen), which he greatly admired as a political statement.

The church is characterised by its octagonal central nave, the longest Gothic nave in Central Europe (22 metres wide).

The towers were damaged several times during the Thirty Years' War in the 17th century; in the following century, the church was rebuilt in Baroque style.

There are other cannonballs of the same vintage embedded in the Church of Our Lady of the Angels at the castle (see p. 161).

LEGEND OF THE DEVIL'S GRIMACE

According to legend, when the vast vault was completed, the church architect (possibly Vít Hedvábný) burned the wooden scaffolding (the normal method of striking scaffolding in the Middle Ages).

Many people expected the roof to fall in, but in the smoke and falling debris some saw the Devil's grimacing face. It was claimed that when the architect noticed the Devil, he fled and committed suicide. The Devil took his soul but left the church standing.

REMAINS OF THE CITY WALLS

Prague has been surrounded with several different walls built during the course of its 1,000-year history: the first fortifications were the strongholds of Šárka, Závist, Butovice, Hostivař, Prague Castle and Vyšehrad.

In the 9th century, under the Přemyslid rulers, Prague Castle and Vyšehrad were protected by simple stone walls, strengthened here and there with wooden palisades.

In the early 12th century, the Romanesque walls were completed around the castle and a number of gates added.

A century later, King Václav I (Přemysl Wenceslas I) ordered the construction of ramparts around the Old Town. Stretching about 4 kilometres in all, they crossed the Vltava and encircled what are now Národní, Na příkopě and Revoluční streets, then ran down to the river.

Emperor Charles IV, who founded the New Town, built the Gothic enclosure from Vyšehrad to Karlov that was extended in the direction of Sokolovská, Mezibranská and Wilsonova streets to rejoin the river at Těšnov.

He was the ruler who built the Hunger Wall (Hladová zeď) that separates the Kinsky Garden from Petřin and formed part of the ramparts of Malá Strana and Hradčany.

These fortifications were rebuilt several times. On the last occasion, a section known as Mariánské hradby was built in the Baroque style of the Vltava (via Letná along the street Na Valech) to Pohořelec, then down the Petřin hill to the river. Of this section, only the Písecká gate can still be seen.

After the Thirty Years' War (1618–48), Vyšehrad was turned into a fortress with bastions and casemates in its massive walls that have been preserved, along with three gates.

All these fortifications have gradually lost their function, starting with those of the Old Town which had no meaning after the construction of the New Town.

Most of these walls were demolished in the 19th century.

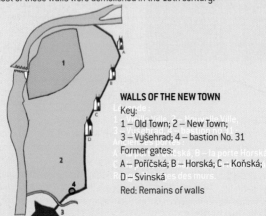

WALLS OF THE NEW TOWN
Key:
1 – Old Town; 2 – New Town;
3 – Vyšehrad; 4 – bastion No. 31
Former gates:
A – Poříčská; B – Horská; C – Koňská;
D – Svinská
Red: Remains of walls

REMAINS OF THE GOTHIC WALLS

Horská
• Tram: 7, 18, 24, Albertov stop

> *Last traces
> of the 1350
> rampart*

Between 1348 and 1350, in an attempt to strengthen the city's defences against prospective attackers, Charles IV had the 3,430-metre-long Gothic walls built around the New Town. From the right bank of the Vltava to Těšnov, they ran up to what is now Prague Main Station, followed Mezibranská and Sokolská streets as far as Karlov and then continued down to the Botič stream to rejoin the fortifications of Vyšehrad (see p. 165).

Only a small section of these Gothic walls remains, between Karlov and Na Slupi Street: this includes former bastion No. 31, now converted into a literary café.

For more on Prague's city walls, see p. 106.

DOG ON FIRE IN HORSKÁ STREET

Behind the fortifications lies the narrow and steeply winding Horská Street, which has long had a bad reputation. Its flights of steps run alongside Ztracenka and Folimanka parks.

According to legend, the spectre of a black dog on fire roams through this inhospitable place at night-time.

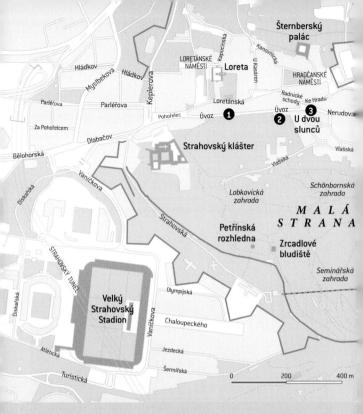

MALÁ STRANA

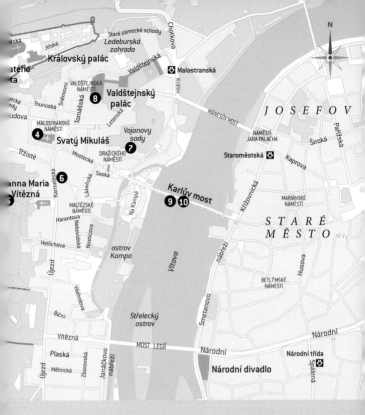

AT THE STONE COLUMN ❶

Úvoz 160/24
• Tram: 12, 22, Malostranské náměstí or Pohořelec stop

Fresco of the miracle of White Mountain

The house at No. 160/24 Úvoz Street, known as U kamenného sloupu (At the Stone Column), belonged to the painter Christian Luna, who contributed to the decoration of the pilgrimage church at White Mountain (see p. 192).

(see p. 192)

This explains why the mural on the façade of the house is a reproduction of the miraculous engraving with whose help the imperial army defeated the troops of the "Winter King" of Bohemia, Frederick the Elector Palatine, at the Battle of White Mountain in 1620.

The house takes its name from the stone column that adorns the façade on which a Madonna reposes. The two corners of the house are also decorated with stucco busts: the left is the Moon deity whose name is a subtle reminder of the house owner; the right represents the Sun. During the day, these two busts are alternately illuminated or plunged into obscurity by the play of light and shade. Remarkably, the shadows falling on the column indicate the first and last hours of the day.

Renowned photographer Josef Sudek lived in this house from 1959 until his death in 1976. His friends, such as the poet Jaroslav Seifert, Nobel Prize for Literature, and the painter Jan Zrzavý, used to meet there.

AT THE GOLDEN APPLE

Úvoz 1
• Tram: 12, 22, Malostranské náměstí or Pohořelec stop

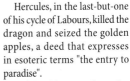

Towards the garden of the Hesperides

U zlatého jablka (At the Golden Apple) – the name of the house at No. 1 Úvoz Street, on the final stage of the esoteric Royal Way – is a clear reference to the Hesperides and the golden apples of Greek mythology.

The three Hesperides, Hespere, Aegle and Erytheia – the daughters of Night in some legends, the daughters of Atlas and Hesperis in others – lived in a fabulous orchard, the garden of the Hesperides at the western edge of the world (probably on the coasts of Spain or Morocco – some consider the name Spain to be derived from Hesperis), which was owned by Hera.

Hera, sister–wife of Zeus, protector of women and goddess of marriage (identified with Juno in Roman mythology), entrusted them to watch over the golden apples in the garden she had given them, as well as enlisting the help of the dragon Ladon.

Hercules, in the last-but-one of his cycle of Labours, killed the dragon and seized the golden apples, a deed that expresses in esoteric terms "the entry to paradise".

For the alchemists, the apples of the Hesperides symbolise the mastery of the Great Work that leads them to the philosopher's stone.

The dragon Ladon had a hundred heads and spoke many languages: an allegory of the great number of philosophers who entered this magical garden to seek out its treasures.

Through its name the dragon is linked with the Titan Leto (Latin: Latona), meaning "hidden, invisible", a reference to the occult nature of the alchemical Great Work that not everyone can attain.

SYMBOLISM OF THE TWO SUNS

Nerudova ulice 47
• Tram: 22, 17, Malostranské náměstí stop

> **Where
> the choice
> must be made**

The house at the junction of Úvoz and Neruda streets, U dvou slunců (At the Two Suns), features an enigmatic cartouche, the upper part of which shows two faces in profile looking in opposite directions. Between them the face of a long-haired man overlooks the golden reliefs of two suns.

The location of this cartouche is particularly interesting: to the right the road leads to the castle, where the exoteric Royal Way ends (see p. 16). Heading towards the "Evening Star" via Úvoz street, a straight line to the west leads to Hvězda (Star Summer Palace, see p. 194), where Venus shines in the dark sky and the esoteric Royal Way ends.

So the cartouche is a true symbol of the choice that can be made at this stage of the Royal Way: note that the two suns (symbolising the purpose of the path) are not identical, each face being slightly different. But they show no preference for which direction to take. It is up to each individual to decide which path to choose.

Following this logic we can better understand the role of the central figure, who is actually the god Mercury, unstable but astute and a vital element in the alchemical process.

Under the suns are a shell and a smaller frame enclosing the letters IHS and a flower with four petals, like a star or cross, and below that a small burning heart.

The letters IHS refer not only to the salvationist role of Christ expressed by the illustrious title *Iesus Homini Salvator* (Jesus Saviour of Mankind), but also to a deeper meaning of the sign itself: IHS also stands for *in hoc signo* (in this sign), an interpretation confirmed by the star or cross directly above the letter H. Unlike the famous sign of the Roman Emperor Constantine (who is reputed to have seen a cross inscribed in the sky with the words *in hoc signo vinces*, showing him the way forward to win the battle he was engaged in), this one is missing *vinces* (conquer): in the choices we make we can indeed still win or lose, it is up to us to choose. The first path is exoteric and leads to fame and glory. The other is esoteric and leads to philosophical and spiritual humility.

For more information on Prague's Royal Way, see p. 16.

BOLLARDS IN MALOSTRANSKÉ SQUARE ❹

In front of Liechtenstein Palace
Malostranské Square
• Tram: 12, 22, Malostranské náměstí stop

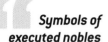

Symbols of executed nobles

Of all the bollards in Prague, the most original are those at the top of Malostranské Square in front of Liechtenstein Palace, which currently houses the Music Faculty of the Prague Academy of Performing Arts (HAMU). Designed in 1993 by sculptor Karel Nepraš (1932–2002), they represent the 27 Czech nobles executed on 21 June 1621 in Old Town Square (see p. 48 for another trace of them).

An incident in 1618 known as the second defenestration of Prague triggered the open hostility of the largely Protestant Czech nobility against the power of the Catholic Habsburgs, and on a larger scale the Thirty Years' War (1618–48) in Europe. The routing of the Protestant armies at the Battle of White Mountain on 8 November 1620 marked the end of the Bohemian Estates' hopes of independence for a long time. The Counter-Reformation was getting into full swing and the Protestant Czechs, including Jan Ámos Komenský (Comenius), were forced to convert or go into exile.

The 27 victims were put to death by Mydlář, the public executioner, who used four swords to finish the job, which took him from 5am to 9.30pm. A dozen nobles and two powerful burghers were beheaded, the rest of them were hanged … with the exception of Dr Jesenius, whose tongue was torn out before his execution. Ferdinand II had the heads of the most illustrious victims displayed on the east tower of Charles Bridge.

The site of the bollards was not chosen at random: the palace belonged to Karel of Liechtenstein, who as imperial governor in Bohemia after the Battle of White Mountain had ordered the executions to punish the leaders of the Protestant rebellion.

GHOSTS OF MALÁ STRANA

Liechtenstein Palace (U bílého medvěda: At the White Bear) was acquired by Karel of Lichtenstein, responsible for the infamous executions of the Czech Protestant nobles who had opposed forced conversion to Catholicism after the Battle of White Mountain. It is alleged that after his death Lidvina his, wife, held orgies in which the Devil took her off to Hell.

The house at No. 11, U zeleného vozu (At the Green Wagon), in Malá Strana marketplace (Tržiště) is said to be a former prison. It has two rooms, one above the other, where the veiled ghost of a man sometimes appears wearing a red hooded coat and old-fashioned boots.

Generations of owners of this house have encountered him at dawn.

CHURCH OF ST NICHOLAS: PENULTIMATE STAGE OF PRAGUE'S ALCHEMICAL PATH

The name of the church just opposite the 27 bollards of Malostranské Square comes from the Greek Nikolaos, which is made up of the words *nikós* (winner) and *láos* (stone): following the logic of Prague's initiatory journey from Malá Strana to the castle, the Church of St Nicholas is the penultimate step before "winning the stone" (the philosopher's stone, that is).

In this alchemical sense, the church dome recalls the upper half of the "imperial globe", similar to the alchemical sign for the world, with the tower representing the royal sceptre. The tower and dome are exactly the same height.

MUSEUM OF THE INFANT JESUS OF PRAGUE ❺

Church of Our Lady Victorious
Karmelitská ulice
• Open: Monday to Saturday, 9.30am–5.30pm; Sunday 1pm–6pm
• Admission free
• Tram: 12, 22, Hellichova stop

> **Symbolism of the colours of Baby Jesus' robes**

The universally known Infant Jesus of Prague is a wax figure dating from the Spanish Renaissance and kept in the Church of Our Lady Victorious. Polyxena von Pernstein, Princess of Lobkowicz (1567–1642), donated it to the church in 1628. She inherited it from her Spanish-born mother, which explains the particular veneration for the figure in the Spanish-speaking world. It was very soon attributed with miraculous powers and people began to shower it with gifts. These included the precious robes that the figure is dressed in for the various religious holidays: Maria Theresa of Austria is thought to have stitched one outfit herself, and the government of North Viet Nam even offered a set of jewellery during the Communist era.

On display in the first-floor museum are around a hundred robes (some unfinished or unwearable), among other clothing. The task of dressing the figure is entrusted to the Carmelite nuns of the Monastery of the Infant Jesus of Prague, who choose outfits according to their liturgical calendar.

Four basic colours are used:

White: the colour of the religious ceremony, purity and holiness, to celebrate Easter and Christmas;

Red: the colour of blood and fire, but also the royal colour for Holy Week, Pentecost and the feast of the Holy Cross;

Purple: the colour symbolising repentance for Lent and Advent;

Green: the colour of life and hope for all periods between these feasts.

During a king's coronation, the Infant Jesus is typically dressed in a royal robe covered with an ermine mantle.

On the most special occasions, He also wears other colours:

Pink: the colour of inner joy, sometimes used for the third Sunday of Advent and the fourth Sunday of Lent;

Gold: the colour of ceremony, which sometimes replaces another colour;

Blue: sometimes used for weddings.

BAS-RELIEF OF A TRIPLE HANDSHAKE ❻

Karmelitská 18
• Tram: 22, 9, 12, Hellichova stop

At No. 18 Karmelitská Street you can see a strange house sign: three linked forearms, shaking each other's hands. This is the Masonic symbol of brotherhood and unity. It also recalls the special Freemasons' greeting.

> *Masonic symbols as house sign*

OTHER MASONIC HANDSHAKES

This symbolic handshake is found in two other Prague streets: at No. 3 Na Zderaze and No. 73 Vinohradská.

THE MASONIC SALUTE

Freemasons salute each other by shaking hands in a distinctive manner. By pressing with their thumb, they indicate their rank. Using the tip of the thumb of the right hand, an apprentice will lightly touch the first knuckle of the other person's right index finger three times: two rapid touches and one long one. A companion will do the same, but will use his right thumb to touch the first knuckle of the other person's middle finger five times: two rapid touches, a long one, and two more rapid ones. A master will do likewise, but with seven touches: four rapid ones and three long ones.

MASONIC SYMBOLS

The square and compass are other important Masonic symbols: examples can easily be seen at No. 7 Janáček embankment (Janáčkovo nábřeží) and at No. 35 Karmelitská, No. 53 Lublaňská, No. 1 Vejvodova and No. 22 Vinohradská streets.

NEARBY

INAUGURAL MEETING OF CZECH FREEMASONRY ❼

The first Freemasons' meeting in the Czech lands, initiated by the French and Saxon troops who occupied Prague in 1741, is thought to have been held at the house of a nobleman called Karel David. Known as U kamenného zvonku (At the Little Stone Bell), the house is at No. 10 Dražickěho Square. The men behind the creation of the Czech Lodges were allegedly the Count of Belle-Isle, Marshal of France, and Count Frederick Augustus Rutowski (illegitimate son of the Polish King Augustus II and Grand Master of the Grand Lodge of Upper Saxony, based in Dresden), commander of the Saxons. According to some sources, the Masonic initiation activities revived the former activities of Count F. A. Sporck (see p. 122).

FREEMASONRY IN BOHEMIA: FROM THE FAUST HOUSE TO ALFONS MUCHA

The first Bohemian Masonic Lodge is thought to have been founded on 24 June 1726 in Prague at the palace of Count František Antonín Sporck (Franz Anton von Sporck, 1662–1738) in the presence of Anthony Sayer, Grand Master of the Grand Lodge of England. It seems to have been called U tří hvězd (At the Three Stars), although this is not certain. Count Sporck was the archetypal freethinker of 18th-century Bohemia: he contested the conservative policies of the Counter-Reformation and the detrimental effects of the old legal system, as well as being a great philanthropist and patron.

In 1761, Jan Christoph Konrad de Nitzky and the Governor of the Old Town, Václav François Vernier, founded a Lodge organised along Rosicrucian lines and called it U černé růže (At the Black Rose). They also studied and practised alchemy.

The story goes that for some time alchemical research was conducted in the Masonic Lodge that met in the so-called Faust House (in Karlovo náměstí) under the direction of alchemist Karel Mladota of Solopysky.

The French officers who, in the mid-18th century, helped Bavaria in its fight against the Habsburgs also initiated a few Czech nobles into Freemasonry. The founding of the Prague Lodge, U tří korun (At the Three Crowns), was primarily due to the French Count de Belle-Isle (Charles-Louis-Auguste Fouquet, 1684–1761). However, Count Frederick Augustus Rutowsky, commander of the Saxon troops who invaded the Czech lands, also introduced Masonic principles to Bohemia.

During the early days of her reign, Empress Maria Theresa was opposed to Freemasonry and fought against its influence, although her husband Francis of Lorraine was himself a member of the Grand Lodge of London.

At that time, there were two Lodges in Prague: U tří korunovaných hvezd (At the Three Crowned Stars) and U tří korunovaných sloupu (At the Three Crowned Columns). Joseph Albert Count Hodicky of Hodice, Joseph

Emanuel Count Canal de Malabaila, Count Hugo von Salm-Reifferscheidt and Ignác Antonín Born (Ignaz von Born, one of the founders of scientific research in Bohemia) were among the eminent Czech Freemasons there. Later, under Joseph II, the activities and development of the Masonic Lodges were more or less tolerated.

In the 19th century, Josef Dobrovský, a renowned linguist who together with Josef Jungmann set down the rules of Czech grammar, were also prominent members.

The best-known figures in the history of Czech Freemasonry, besides those already mentioned, are the painter Alfons Mucha, the politicians Jan Masaryk and Edvard Beneš, and Dr Ladislav Syllaba who was Grand Master of the Grand Lodge of Czechoslovakia.

Under the Nazi and Communist regimes, Freemasonry was banned in Czechoslovakia and the Lodges fell "dormant". Since the Velvet Revolution in 1989, they have been experiencing a revival.

THE SUN CHARIOT: TWO OR FOUR HORSES? APOLLO OR HELIOS?

In the Baroque Main Hall of Wallenstein Palace (open to visitors at weekends), the central ceiling fresco shows Albrecht von Wallenstein as Mars, the Roman god of war, triumphant on the Sun chariot pulled by four horses.

The Sun chariot is a mythological concept according to which Helios (or sometimes Apollo) pulls the Sun through the sky attached to his chariot.

Helios, the Greek personification of the Sun and light, was the son of the Titan Hyperion and the Titanide Theia. Apollo, the god of light and the Sun, is sometimes confused with Helios, the personification of the Sun. One of their distinguishing characteristics is the number of horses drawing the Sun chariot: Helios' chariot has four horses, as here, whereas Apollo's has only two (as in the famous fresco by Guido Reni in Rome's Casino dell'Aurora – Dawn Pavilion – see *Secret Rome* in this series of guidebooks).

ASTRONOMICAL CORRIDOR
AT WALLENSTEIN PALACE

- Palace open Saturday and Sunday, 10am–4pm
- Astronomical corridor usually closed to the public
- Metro: Klárov; Tram: 17, 22, Malostranská or Klárov stop

*Palace
of the Zodiac*

Beginning in 1623, Albrecht von Wallenstein (1583–1634), Duke of Friedland and Mecklenburg, had the vast palace built that bears his name. Throughout his life he was obsessed with astrology: the great astronomer Johannes Kepler drew up several horoscopes for him, although Wallenstein also had a personal astrologer, the renowned Italian Giovanni Battista Zenno, known as Seni.

To satisfy this passion, Wallenstein built an astronomical and astrological corridor linking the north and south wings of his palace. Unfortunately closed to the public, the corridor is a unique example of Czech Mannerist Baroque art in its decoration, layout and certain idiosyncratic features.

The vault is indeed a celestial sphere, the walls representing the terrestrial world. It is divided into seven sections corresponding to the number of planets known at the time, according to which Kepler had made Wallenstein's horoscopes.

On the walls, the 12 signs of the zodiac are shown as an allegory in association with the planets: right at the top is the Moon in the form of the goddess Diana with the sign of Cancer at her side. Below are Mercury-Hermes and the signs of Gemini and Virgo, followed by Venus, depicted in the form of Aphrodite, with the signs of Taurus and Libra. In the centre of this procession are the Sun and Leo and below that Mars-Ares and the signs of Aries and Scorpio. The sixth planet is Jupiter-Zeus with the signs of Pisces and Sagittarius. Finally, at the bottom, are Saturn-Cronus and the signs of Aquarius and Capricorn.

Far from being merely decorative, this cycle of frescoes had a real Hermetic sense – according to the theory long believed to have been handed down from Hermes Trismegistus, for whom "what is above is like what is below" and who gave his name to hermeticism – in that it allowed the celestial energy as represented on the ceiling fresco to be more strongly attracted.

WALLENSTEIN'S HOROSCOPE

Johannes Kepler is said to have had no special knowledge of astrology, although he was extremely interested in the subject and raised its standing. In 1601, he published *De Fundamentis Astrologiae Certioribus* (Concerning the More Certain Fundamentals of Astrology).

In 1608 the first version of the legendary horoscope for Albrecht von Wallenstein appeared anonymously. Although not all the details were correct, the horoscope made some accurate predictions. In corrections made in 1624 and 1628 while he was in Wallenstein's service, Kepler warned that he could be defeated by the Danes as well as the Swedes in the near future. He also predicted the rise of an anti-Wallenstein movement in 1632 and a crisis in his personal life in 1634. Despite urging by Wallenstein's entourage, he refused to make forecasts for the period after 1634 because the stars were against his master.

All the predictions proved accurate as the duke was assassinated in 1634. The astrological chart shown below, known as Kepler's Wallenstein Horoscope, is typical of the Baroque period.

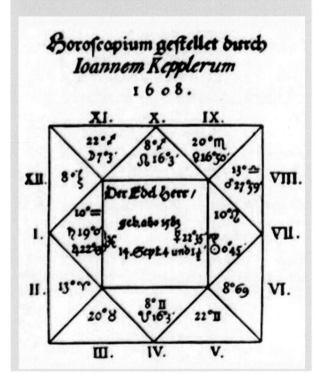

PRINCIPLES OF THE WALLENSTEIN HOROSCOPE

The date of birth is inscribed in the central square. Running round the square in an anti-clockwise direction are 12 triangles representing the 12 astrological houses.

Within the triangles, the position of the signs of the zodiac and the planets are indicated at the time of birth of the person concerned.

The positive sign that Kepler saw here was the conjunction of Saturn with Jupiter in the 1st house and Mercury with the Sun in the 7th.

Similarly, the position of the Sun is at the cardinal point of the autumnal equinox. Thus the planets Saturn, Jupiter, Mercury and Venus in this horoscope are reciprocally related to favourable astrological aspects (angles the planets make with each other and other points of interest, known as conjunctions, oppositions, sextiles and trines). The less favourable aspects of Kepler's horoscope correspond to the position of the Moon in the 12th house because astrologers say that the Moon is "in exile" in Capricorn.

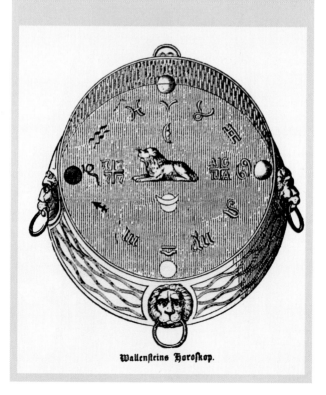

Wallensteins Horoskop.

THE MOOR'S CAT-O'-NINE-TAILS

Charles Bridge
• Metro: Malostranská; Tram: 12, 22, Malostranské náměstí stop

> **The Trinitarian mission to free Christian prisoners**

Just opposite the statue of St John of Nepomuk on Charles Bridge is a group of carvings by the celebrated Prague sculptor F. M. Brokof (1714). They include St John of Matha standing on a rock with his wrists unchained, at his side Félix of Valois and at his feet the hermit Ivan, representing the country's saints. At the foot of the statue, Christian prisoners in a dungeon with an iron gate are guarded by a Moor and his dog.

The sculpture was commissioned by the Trinitarian Order, founded in the 12th century by St John of Matha and Félix of Valois, hence their presence in the group. The Order's mission was to ransom the Christians taken captive by the Moors, represented here by the Moorish figure. In the early 18th century, Prague was still under the threat of Turkish invasion.

By leaning over the parapet of the bridge, you can see the whip carefully hidden behind the Moor's back, a clear reminder of the relationship between the prisoners and their masters.

WHO ARE THE TRINITARIANS (MATHURINS)?

The Order of the Most Holy Trinity for the Redemption of Captives (Latin: *Ordo Sanctissimae Trinitatis redemptionis captivorum,* O.SS.T. for short), known as the Trinitarians or Mathurins (after St John of Matha), is a Roman Catholic religious order founded in 1194 by John of Matha and Félix of Valois.

The Order's original mission was to ransom the Christians taken captive by the Moors, and it still helps prisoners and captives of all kinds.

The Trinitarian emblem is a mosaic dating from 1210, which depicts Jesus freeing two chained captives, a black Moor and a white Christian, as St Jean of Matha saw them in a vision on 28 January 1193. The mosaic, given by Pope Innocent III to St John of Matha, is still in Rome on the church pediment at the hospice of San Tommaso in Formis.

ST JOHN OF NEPOMUK'S HALO

Charles Bridge
• Metro: Malostranská; Tram: 12, 22, Malostranské náměstí stop

J ohn of Nepomuk, the son of Welflin (or Wölflin), a burgher of Pomuk, is a Czech saint whose cult spread well beyond Bohemia in the Baroque period.

> **Why is John of Nepomuk crowned with five stars?**

According to the *Chronica regum Romanorum* by the Austrian chronicler Thomas Ebendorfer (died 1464) and the *Annals Bohemorum* (1541), John was priest confessor to Queen Sophia, who had married Wenceslas IV in 1389. John had criticised the king and refused to betray the confessions of the queen, whom Wenceslas suspected of adultery. He was tortured and thrown into the Vltava in 1393 on the north side of the bridge, between the sixth and seventh pillars, where a plaque commemorates the deed.

John of Nepomuk, like the Virgin Mary, is the only saint to bear a halo of five stars rather than a traditional halo. According to tradition, this halo symbolises the five wounds of Christ and the five letters of the Latin word *TACUI* ("I kept silent" – referring to his silence under torture). The stars are also meant as a reminder of the stars glittering on the Vltava waters that helped to locate the mutilated body of the saint washed up by the current.

Finally, on some nights the reflection of the Northern Crown (*Corona Borealis*) constellation can be seen on the surface of the river – this may also have contributed to the legend of the starred halo.

The starred halo was accorded to the saint after his canonisation by Pope Benedict XIII in 1729. Previously, he had a garland of stars.

In 1724, doctors present at the autopsy of the remains of the saint's body recorded the fact that his tongue had been preserved intact. It was placed in a reliquary. A new autopsy in 1972 showed that it was not the tongue but remnants of brain tissue. John of Nepomuk's body and "tongue" are now in a tomb at St Vitus Cathedral in Hradčany.

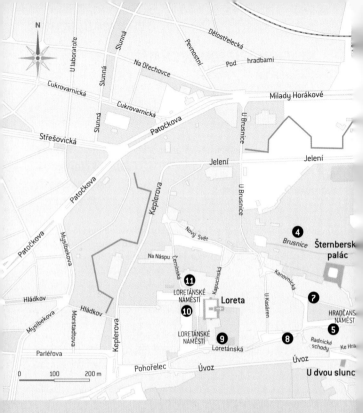

HRADČANY (CASTLE)

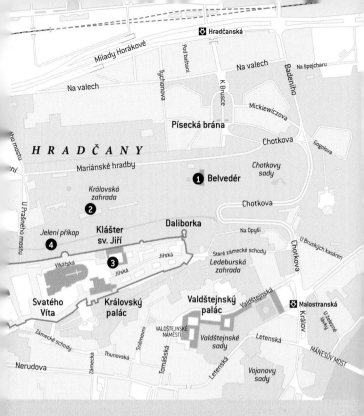

HERMETIC SYMBOLISM OF THE BELVEDERE ❶

Královská zahrada (Royal Garden)
• Tram: 22, Letohrádek královny Anny stop

> *Occult architectural gem*

Built by Emperor Ferdinand I, the Royal Summer Palace of Queen Anne (also known as the Belvedere) is one of the most beautiful Renaissance buildings in Prague. Like much of the city's architecture it features many references to alchemy, in which Ferdinand I took a great interest (the physician and alchemist Paracelsus, who established the role of chemistry in medicine, even dedicated several treatises to him).

The Summer Palace is designed like a Roman villa, encircled by an arcade with 36 Ionic columns set 3 metres apart. There are 6 columns on each side and 14 to the front and back of the rectangular building, which is oriented on a north-south axis. Narrative bas-reliefs in stone, 12 and 4 on their respective sides of the building, are set between the arches above the capital of each of these columns.

The 12 bas-reliefs are related to the signs of the zodiac and the months of the year. The others recall the four constituent elements (Earth, Air, Water, Fire), and the four cardinal virtues (Prudence, Justice, Fortitude and Temperance).

Totalling 32 (12+12+4+4), a perfect Kabbalistic number, the upper bas-reliefs tell the story of "32 ways that lead to Wisdom".

As the bases of the columns each bear a vertical bas-relief, the Belvedere has 72 in all (32+40), a figure that Kabbalists attribute to the number of letters in the explicit name of God, which is Shem-ham-forash (see p. 66). The upper bas-reliefs of the north, south and west walls of the palace are essentially Graeco-Roman mythological motifs, while the lower ones are dedicated to the struggles of the heroes of antiquity.

Two interior reliefs at the end of the west wall show the symbolic battle with the dragon: to the left Jason the Argonaut at Colchis in his quest for the Golden Fleece, and to the right the hero Cadmus fighting the dragon of the Greek god Ares. This is an allegory of alchemists' treaties symbolising their

work in the transmutation of matter. Various reliefs depict the interventions of Zeus in the presence of most of the gods of Olympus. Near the former entrance on the same side is a relief of Vulcan and Mercury, the two protagonists of work on base metals. The former entrance bears the personification of Furor (symbolising *prima materia* or first matter) and the god Janus holding two keys in his hand. This not only confirms his erstwhile function as custodian of the entrance to the Belvedere, but the two keys also symbolically recall the two possible routes to the alchemical Great Work (the dry and the wet), which makes it possible to "open the door to the closed palace of the king" or find the philosopher's stone. This hoped-for success is symbolised by an adjacent relief of Aeneas harvesting crops.

The bases of the four columns on the side walls feature bas-reliefs of the Labours of Hercules, synonymous with the alchemical process. In this way the mythical hero symbolically endorses this construction.

The upper reliefs on the south side depict mythological hunting scenes of antiquity (Meleager, the leader of the Calydonian boar hunt, Atalanta the huntress), as well as an amazing scene in which the head of the Calydonian boar is offered as a trophy to Ferdinand I and his sons Maximilian and Ferdinand of Tyrol.

This thematic group of Atalanta's race and the boar hunt is recalled in the renowned work *Atalanta fugiens* by the alchemist and personal physician of Rudolf II, Michael Maier, who probably took part in alchemical experiments at the Belvedere.

In addition, the roof of the building looks like a capsized boat, evoking the notion of *naufragio philosophorum* (philosophical shipwreck): this symbolises the many unsuccessful alchemical experiments that took place here, especially during the reign of Rudolf II.

SGRAFFITI ON THE COURTS

Míčovna, Královská zahrada
(Ball Game Hall, Royal Garden)
• Tram: 22, Pražský hrad stop

Ball Game Hall (Míčovna) is a magnificent Renaissance pavilion built between 1565 and 1569 (during the reign of Ferdinand I) by Bonifaz Wohlmuth in classical style. The hall, on the site of a former shooting range, was the setting for many ball games.

Communists and the Renaissance

The building, burned down during the Liberation of Prague in 1945, was rebuilt in the 1950s during the Communist era but with the addition of a rather unusual detail: while the rest of the building is in Renaissance style, in the third arch to the left, the sculptor J. Wagner replaced the *sgraffito* destroyed by the Germans with a design referring to the Communist five-year plan (*pětiletka*), symbolised by the hammer (industry) and sickle (agriculture).

This is the only surviving element of Socialist Realism to be seen at Prague Castle.

The hall, 68 metres long and 13 metres wide, was a masterpiece of Renaissance architecture. The former *sgraffiti* have been reproduced, personifying the four elements (Earth, Air, Fire, Water), the seven capital virtues (Prudence, Temperance, Charity, Hope, Courage, Justice, Faith) and the liberal arts (Theology, Astronomy, Geometry, Music, Arithmetic, Rhetoric, Dialectic and Grammar).

STATUE OF A DEAD WOMAN ❸

Basilica of St George
Náměstí U Svatého Jiří (St George Square)
Praha 1–Hradčany, 119 08
• Tel: 224 372 434 (castle information centre)
• Tram: 22

At Prague Castle, in the choir of the chapel of the Romanesque Basilica of St George, is a startling figure of a dead woman. Brigita, as she has always been known, is shown with her body decomposed, crawling with frogs, snakes and newts.

Brigita's ghost

According to legend, Brigita was a poor girl from Malá Strana who fell in love with an Italian sculptor who asked her to marry him.

During a long trip abroad, the sculptor agonised over his wife's fidelity.

Meanwhile the young woman had become the victim of some jealous neighbours, who by slandering her managed to convince the sculptor of her infidelity. He killed her and hid her body, but it was discovered and the sculptor confessed his crime. Sentenced to death, he repented and made one last wish: to create a statue of his lover exactly as she was found.

SECRETS OF ST GEORGE'S

The Basilica of St George, founded before 920, is the burial place of the Přemyslid rulers.

In the adjoining chapel is the precious *Passional of the Abbess Kunhuta* (Cunigunde), written in the 12th century by the monk Kolda and illuminated by Beneš, which expressed the medieval alchemical creed in the Czech language for the first time.

According to legend, a crucifix supposedly began to bleed as Přemysl Otakar II, "the king of iron and gold", lay dying after the Battle of Moravské pole (Moravian Field). The whereabouts of this crucifix is unknown.

ALCHEMISTS AT PRAGUE CASTLE

Prague Castle, a city within a city, was exempt from the law, thus attracting a plethora of artisans and charlatans who settled along its ramparts. From the late 14th to the late 16th centuries when, throughout Europe, alchemists, hermeticists, occultists and other followers of the traditional sciences were persecuted by the Roman Catholic Church, they found refuge in Prague, especially during the reign of Rudolf II, who was fascinated by alchemy (see p. 144).

However, it is unlikely that any true alchemists lived in Golden Lane (Zlatá ulička), even if the place had a special significance in the popular imagination. The laboratories of the emperor's alchemists were known to be in the Powder Tower (Mihulka). The lane is probably so named because of the goldsmiths who lived in the little houses built against the ramparts.

Legend has it that Rudolf kept his alchemists locked up in these cottages. When a transmutation took place, the alchemist was supposed to open a shuttered window. Guards armed with halberds patrolled the lane day and night, while some of the alchemists, eager to find the philosopher's stone, grew impatient at not being able to go out and breathe the fresh air of the Stag Moat (Jelení příkop) just outside the city walls. So they asked permission from the emperor, but the park was reserved for the court's most aristocratic guests and it was inconceivable for coarse distillers to be allowed to mingle with the nobles. When permission was refused, the alchemists cut off their hair, destroyed their apparatus and threw it over the ramparts onto the heads of Rudolf's noble guests. They even refused to produce a single nugget of gold.

Faced with this rebellion, the emperor changed his mind and allowed some of the alchemists to take the air in the park: he locked them in metal cages hung on the trees, so they slowly expired of hunger and thirst. The task of the alchemist was sacred and under no circumstances could he abandon the Opus Magnum (Great Work) at any stage of its realisation.

More recently, Gustav Meyrink (see p. 93) wrote in his novel *The Angel of the West Window* that the bears in the Stag Moat "lived on the flesh of the initiates".

In the early 19th century, two alchemists from Golden Lane are said to have manufactured gold, but they suddenly died two days apart: one was a baron from southern Bohemia, the other a former professor of philosophy. It is said that in Golden Lane there used to be a house called U Poslední lucerny (At the Last Lantern), which could only be seen on certain nights of the year.

Ancient tradition also recounts that the first foundation stone of Prague (Praha; prah = threshold) between the visible and invisible worlds was placed there by the Esoteric Order of Asian Monks of Sat-Bhaja.

Franz Kafka lived at number 22 Golden Lane in 1916, at the same time as Polish writer Stanisław Przybyszewski.

The emperor's renown brought various personalities to Prague, such as the English occultist John Dee, the English alchemist Edward Kelley also known as Edward Talbot (who had had his ears cut off as a punishment) and the Pole Michael Sendivogius, who is said to have made several transmutations in the emperor's presence. Impressed, Rudolf II erected a plaque, long gone from the castle walls, that read: "Let anyone else do what the Pole Sendivogius has done."

The celebrated French alchemist Denis Zachaire of Toulouse and his compatriot Nicolas Barnaud also came to Prague, as well as the chemist Oswald Croll or Crollius (indirectly a disciple of Paracelsus), who was famous for his book on precious stones but expelled from Prague for political espionage.

Two of the emperor's physicians were also well-known alchemists: the first, Michael Maier, author of the seminal work *Atalanta fugiens* (1618), is often associated with the Rosicrucian secret society to which he was thought to belong; the other, Martin Ruland, was fascinated by the works of Paracelsus and compiled a very useful dictionary of alchemy, *Lexicon alchemiae*.

The extended group of alchemists, working not only at the castle for the emperor but also for the lords of Rosenberg and Wenceslas Vřesovec, has been called the "Prague School of Alchemy".

The court poet, Mardocheus de Delle from Milan, wrote *Fegefeuer* (Purgatory), which describes the various alchemists.

The empire's mining officials were also involved in work on precious metals and practised the arcane sciences. Lazarus Ercker, for example, wrote an important book on early metallurgy. Mention could also be made of Sebastian Essen who died captive in the castle's White Tower (Bílá věž), and Sebald Schwertzer, from Jáchymov (Joachimsthal) and guest of Rudolf II, who came to enjoy the emperor's patronage and remained in Prague until his death in 1611. He also wrote several alchemical texts.

CODEX GIGAS OR DEVIL'S BIBLE

The *Codex Gigas* (Giant Book) is the largest known medieval manuscript. It is also referred to as the Devil's Bible, on the one hand because there is a large illustration of the Devil inside and on the other because of the legend surrounding its creation. The work contains the Vulgate Bible as well as many historical documents, all written in Latin.

The general consensus is that it was written in the early 13th century in the Benedictine monastery at Podlažice in Bohemia, which was destroyed in the 15th century. The last text to be added is dated 1229.

The codex was later found in the Cistercian monastery at Sedlec near Kutná Hora and was then bought by the Benedictines of Břevnov Monastery. From 1477 to 1593, the book was kept in the library of Broumov Monastery until 1594, when it was bought by Rudolf II. In 1648 during the Thirty Years' War most of the emperor's collections were stolen by the Swedish army, including the *Codex Gigas*, now at the National Library of Sweden in Stockholm.

The codex, 92 cm high, 50 cm wide and 22 cm thick, is bound in a wooden folder covered with leather and metal. It weighs over 75 kg and contains 310 sheets of parchment in perfect condition. Although it originally had 320 sheets made from the skins of 160 donkeys, some were removed for unknown reasons – perhaps because they set down the monastic rules of the Benedictines.

According to a medieval legend, the author of the codex was a monk who broke his vows and was sentenced to be walled up alive. To avoid this terrible punishment, he promised to create the book in one night.

Around midnight, unable to complete this task alone, he addressed a prayer, not to God but to the fallen archangel Lucifer, with whom he made a pact, delivering his soul in exchange for finishing the book.

The work was then completed by Lucifer, and in his gratitude the monk added the image of the Devil. Experts estimate the time it would have taken to write the codex as around 20 years.

VOYNICH MANUSCRIPT: "THE WORLD'S MOST MYSTERIOUS MANUSCRIPT"

Consisting of about 240 vellum pages, the Voynich Manuscript is an illustrated document believed to date from the early 15th century. Although many possible authors have been suggested, nothing about this document is known, from author and content to the language used. It has been described as "the world's most mysterious manuscript".

The text, generally thought to be encoded, has been studied by many professional and amateur cryptographers, including American and British military codebreakers from both world wars. Without success.

This mystery has excited popular imagination, giving rise to the most romantic and fanciful theories.

The Voynich Manuscript, which appears to cover topics such as botany, astrology, astronomy, cosmology, pharmacology and biology, has been attributed to Roger Bacon, the English Franciscan philosopher and polymath (c. 1214–94).

At the end of the 16th century, the manuscript was bought by Emperor Rudolf II to enrich his collection. The first page carries the signature of Jacobus Sinapius of Tepenec, personal physician to the emperor – this renowned Czech alchemist, a specialist in herbal medicine and curator of the Royal Botanic Gardens, was therefore considered as the author.

In the early 17th century, the Voynich Manuscript was in the possession of Jiří Bareš, an obscure Czech alchemist who lived in Prague. On his death, the manuscript passed to his friend Johannes Marcus Marci, then rector of Charles University. A few years later the rector sent the document to Athanasius Kircher, his correspondent and long-time friend (for more on this complex character, see *Secret Rome* in this series of guidebooks).

The manuscript is now named after the 20th-century book dealer who bought it in 1912, Wilfrid M. Voynich, and is in the collection of Yale University's Beinecke Rare Book and Manuscript Library (Connecticut, United States).

RUDOLF II – A MANIC-DEPRESSIVE EMPEROR

Emperor Rudolf II (18 July 1552 – 20 January 1612) was an introvert, a lover of life and the ladies, an erudite scholar of the arts, and a supporter and protector of the occult.

In 1563, the young Rudolf was sent with his brother to the Spanish Court to complete his education. There he was introduced to the work of Hiëronymus Bosch, of whom he became a fervent admirer and keen collector.

On Rudolf's return from Spain, his father appointed him as successor to the monarchy of each of the countries of the Habsburg domain and the Germanic Roman Empire. In 1575, Rudolf was crowned Czech king and designated as the next Holy Roman Emperor.

During the first years of his reign, Rudolf took great pleasure in being in Prague, where he stayed for increasingly lengthy periods. In 1583, he decided to undertake the work required so he could live at the castle permanently and maintain his seat of government there.

During his reign, Prague expanded into a hub of European politics as well as of scientific and artistic life.

Unfortunately, Rudolf's style of government was determined to some extent by mental illness, in his case probably a combination of manic depression and progressive physical paralysis.

Where women were concerned, the emperor preferred short-term relationships, with the exception of his long cohabitation with Catherine Strada. With his various mistresses he had six or seven illegitimate children – it is not known what became of them all.

The most prominent among them was Julius Caesar d'Austria, also mentally ill.

In 1606, taking advantage of the emperor's many relapses, the Habsburg archdukes held a secret meeting in Vienna and set up his younger brother Archduke Matthias as head of the royal family and designated successor to the crown. But the emperor soon discovered the plot and his hatred for his brother increased.

In 1609, Rudolf II issued his famous *Majestätsbrief* (Letter of Majesty), in which he guarantees religious freedom in the Czech lands.

Two years later, while the emperor's mental instability was growing worse, he tried to reassert his widely disputed authority by launching a military campaign with the help of his cousin, Archduke Leopold, Bishop of Passau. Early in 1611 the troops of Passau invaded Bohemia. This was a complete failure and the emperor was forced to abdicate in April.

Nine months later, on 20 January 1612, he died at Prague Castle and was buried in the royal vault of St Vitus Cathedral.

RUDOLF II AND ESOTERICISM

Of all the Habsburg monarchs it was Rudolf II who did the most to protect the occult and the sages devoted to it. Having acquired a taste for alchemy and astrology at the court of Philip II of Spain, he left the government in the hands of his ministers and shut himself up in Prague Castle, where he devoted himself almost exclusively to his favoured studies until the end of his life. It was his personal physicians – first Tadeáš Hájek z Hájku, then Michael Maier and Martin Ruland – who gave him his first lessons in alchemy.

Later he brought to his court the most renowned alchemists of the time: John Dee, Edward Kelley, Michael Sendivogius and Crollius among others. At that time, relays of alchemists worked at the castle and the emperor himself spent time in the laboratories.

For the purpose of his experiments, spagyric and alchemical ingredients were brought to the royal residence: Drosera, a round-leaved plant commonly known as sundew (from the Latin *ros solis*), picked in the morning dew, as well as other more exotic ingredients such as moss growing from the skulls of hanged men.

It is said that Rudolf II alone prepared the philosopher's stone, estimated at the time at 40,000 ducats and which he kept in a flat silver-leaf box covered with red velvet. An eyewitness stated that the box contained a heavy grey powder, similar to ash. After Rudolf's death, the box was stolen by his valet, Kaspar Rucky von Rudz. In the coffin of Rudolf II, three rings were found. One of them was set on the outside with four precious stones (diamond, sapphire, ruby and emerald) and four signs of the zodiac (Capricorn, Libra, Aquarius and Cancer). On the inside of the rings were inscribed the names of four angels (Gabriel, Michael, Uriel and Anael, the last two from the Apocrypha rather than the Bible), accompanied by a magic formula, AGLA, which in the Jewish Kabbalah was often used as the mystic name of God.

The emperor's favourite motto was the acronym ADSIT, which was engraved on one of these magic rings. Some have interpreted these letters to mean *Auxiliante Deo Sum Inimicis Terror* (With God's help I intimidate my enemies), whereas others claim they mean *A Dominus Salus In Tribulatione* (Salvation in tribulation comes from God).

Rudolf was also particularly interested in symbols, as borne out by the collection *Symbola divina et humana I* by Jacob Typotius, Octavian de Strada and Aegidius Sadeler, published with imperial authorisation in Prague in 1601.

Besides alchemy, the emperor also had a keen interest in magic, astrology and the Kabbalah. Several astrologers thus worked at his court, notably Tycho Brahe and Johannes Kepler, and in 1593 the emperor held an audience with the famous Rabbi Judah Loew, creator of the Golem, sharing the secrets of the Jewish Kabbalah.

SECRETS OF THE STAG MOAT ④

Access from Klárov through a small door on a stone terrace in Chotkova Street or from the other side of the moat in Nový svět (New World) lane
- Open 1 April to 31 October
- Tram: 22, Pražský hrad stop

From bear cage to bunker ...

Prague Castle is protected by a natural ravine where the Brusnice stream flows. Known since the Middle Ages as the "Stag Moat" (Jelení příkop), it was a wildlife haven and sometimes deer were even shot from the castle windows. During the two years of French occupation in 1741 and 1742, all the deer were killed and only the name lingered on. However, other animals were kept in cages to amuse the castle residents.

The small windows of the cottages in Golden Lane and Dalibor Tower (Daliborka), once the castle's prison, overlooked the Stag Moat. It is said that one day the alchemists who worked in Golden Lane rebelled because of their low pay and threw their stills and elixirs into the ravine to protest. By way of punishment, Emperor Rudolf II had them thrown in as well, to feed the animals. As the Austrian author Gustav Meyrink wrote, "the bears of the Stag Moat lived on the flesh of the initiates".

According to 18th-century reports, "aerial salt, aerial water, aerial oil" were extracted from this moat. It is said that this miraculous triple mixture based on Prague Castle shale was created by Mladota of Solopysky, a noble known for mysterious alchemical practices with his disciples at the Faust House in Charles Square (Karlovo náměstí, see p. 99).

Only after the Velvet Revolution (1989) was the Stag Moat opened to the public.

In 1951, the Communist regime decided to build a nuclear shelter there. The construction work, with its secret passages near the castle, went on for six years. In 1957, for both financial and strategic reasons, work was stopped on the orders of President Antonín Zápotocký. At the foot of the Stag Moat is the entrance to the concrete bunker, almost opposite Dalibor Tower. Inside is an apartment already prepared for the president, but unfortunately not open to the public.

Powder Bridge (Prašný most), built in the 16th century to link the newly created Royal Garden with the sovereign's residence, spanned the Stag Moat. Today the path enters an 84-metre brick tunnel built under this bridge by architect Josef Pleskot on the initiative of President Václav Havel. You can see the Brusnice stream flowing under the floor gratings.

The little white house in the upper reaches of the moat (towards Nový svět) was the home of the former bear keeper: bears donated to President Masaryk in 1918 by members of the Czechoslovak Legions were kept here until the 1950s. Today, only their cages survive.

NEARBY

OLDEST SUNDIAL IN PRAGUE ❺
Schwarzenberg Palace, Hradčanské náměstí 2/185
• Tram: 22, Pražský hrad stop

On the chimney of Schwarzenberg Palace and visible from Nerudova Street is the oldest sundial in Prague, dating from the mid-16th century.

It was in this very palace that the celebrated court astronomer Tycho Brahe died of a burst bladder, 11 days after attending an imperial banquet: he is thought to have refused to leave the emperor's table to relieve himself as he felt that would be a breach of etiquette.

BAS-RELIEF OF THE ROTATING STAR ❻

Archdiocese of Prague - Hradčanské náměstí 16 (Hradčany Square)
• Tram: 22, Pražský Hrad stop

> **Mysterious sign at the Archbishop's Palace**

The Archbishop's Palace, between Prague Castle and Sternberg Palace, is the current seat of the Archbishop of Prague, replacing the Old Priory near St Vitus Cathedral and the house known as Bishop's Court in Malá Strana, now occupied by the Ministry of Finance.

On both sides of the entrance columns are striking bas-reliefs representing a "rotating star", an aggregate of the swastika (details opposite) and the hexagram (see following double-page spread).

During the Hussite rebellions the second seat of the archbishop, the former Bishop's Court, was burned to the ground. Archbishop Conrad of Vechta (1413–21) defected to the Hussite camp and the seat remained vacant for 140 years from 1421. In 1561, Antonín Brus of Mohelnice, who was also Grand Master of the Knights of the Cross with the Red Star (1561–80), became Archbishop of Prague. Following a donation on 5 October 1561 by Emperor Ferdinand I, the Church received the house near Prague Castle that had once belonged to the nobleman Florián Griespek of Griesbach as the seat of Prague archdiocese and residence of its representative.

ROTATING STAR SYMBOL: A HEXAGRAM AND A SWASTIKA ...

The rotating star is a compound of two symbols: the hexalpha (or hexagram) itself, a six-pointed star made up of two locked equilateral triangles; and the swastika, whose four arms bend at right angles in the same rotary direction.

The two triangles of the hexagram express interlinked celestial energy (marked by the triangle pointing upwards, traditionally emerald green) and the Earth's electromagnetic force (indicated by the triangle pointing downwards, traditionally bright red), a union of spirit and matter made possible by the power generated by the two forces (designated by the swastika).

It is very important to distinguish between swastika and *sauvastika*. The *sauvastika* rotates to the left – it is considered regressive and sinister by Eastern religions and the peoples of Western antiquity, who saw the swastika, rotating to the right, as a positive and evolutionary symbol. Adolf Hitler and his followers appropriated this symbol that had been sacred for thousands of years and turned it into an evil *sauvastika*.

It is indeed the direction in which the swastika and *sauvastika* are rotating that determines their direct meaning: right-hand (positive, solar) symbolises universal evolution and is typified by the swastika adopted by Charlemagne; left-hand (negative, lunar or anti-clockwise) signals that the more immediate context is to subject the timeless and sacred to profane space and time, and is then represented by the *sauvastika* adapted by Hitler.

The arms of the swastika, formed by four Greek gammas (which is why it is also known as the gamma cross), are a symbol of universal action and the ongoing transformation of the Life-Energy to Life-Consciousness. In this sense, it has always accompanied the saviours of humanity such as Christ. Christ is depicted in the ancient Roman catacombs at the centre of a spiral-shaped swastika, as the representative of the spiritual core where God is present.

So is this the message of this circumgyratory hexagram carved on the façade of the Archbishop's Palace in Prague: that universal life sprang from Christ, has evolved in the faith, and that it is to Christ we must return at the end of time, in other words at the end of the present cycle where everyone and everything is constantly evolving?

More about the symbolism of the hexagram on the following double-page spread.

THE STAR HEXAGRAM: A MAGICAL TALISMAN?

The hexagram – also known as the Star of David or the Shield of David – comprises two interlaced equilateral triangles, one pointing upwards and the other downwards. It symbolises the combination of man's spiritual and human nature. The six points correspond to the six directions in space (north, south, east and west, together with zenith and nadir) and also refer to the complete universal cycle of the six days of creation (the seventh day being when the Creator rested). Hence, the hexagram became the symbol of the macrocosm (its six angles of 60° totalling 360°) and of the union between mankind and its creator. If, as laid down in the Old Testament (*Deuteronomy* 6:4–9), the hexagram (*mezuzah* in Hebrew) is often placed at the entrance to a Jewish home, it was also adopted as an amulet by Christians and Muslims. So it is far from being an exclusively Jewish symbol. In both the Koran (38:32 et seq.) and *The Thousand and One Nights*, it is described as an indestructible talisman that affords God's blessing and offers total protection against the spirits of the natural world, the djinns. The hexagram also often appears in the windows and pediments of Christian churches, as a symbolic reference to the universal soul. In this case, that soul is represented by Christ – or, sometimes, by the pair of Christ (upright triangle) and the Virgin (inverted triangle); the result of the interlacing of the two is God the Father Almighty. The hexagram is also found in the mediated form of a lamp with six branches or a six-section rose window.

Although present in the synagogue of Capernaum (third century AD), the hexagram does not really make its appearance in rabbinical literature until 1148 – in the *Eshkol Hakofer* written by the Karaite* scholar Judah Ben Elijah. In Chapter 242 its mystical and apotropaic (evil-averting) qualities are described, with the actual words then often being engraved on amulets: "And the names of the seven angels were written on the *mazuzah* … The Everlasting will protect you and this symbol called the Shield of David contains, at the end of the *mezuzah*, the written name of all the angels."

In the thirteenth century the hexagram also became an attribute of one of the seven magic names of Metatron, the angel of the divine presence associated with the archangel Michael (head of the heavenly host and the closest to God the Father).

The identification of Judaism with the Star of David began in the Middle Ages. In 1354 King Karel IV of Bohemia granted the Jewish community of Prague the privilege of putting the symbol on their banner. The Jews embroidered a gold star on a red background to form a standard that became known as the Flag of King David (*Maghen David*) and was adopted as the official symbol of Jewish synagogues. By the nineteenth century, the symbol had spread throughout the Jewish community. Jewish mysticism has it that the origin of the hexagram was directly linked with the flowers that adorn the *menorah***: irises with six petals. For those who believe this origin, the hexagram came directly from the hands of the God of Israel, the six-petal iris not only reassembling the Star of David in general form but also being associated with the people of Israel in the *Song of Songs*.

As well as offering protection, the hexagram was believed to have magical powers. This reputation originates in the famous *Clavicula Salomonis* (Key of Solomon), a grimoire (textbook of magic) attributed to Solomon himself but, in all likelihood, produced during the Middle Ages. The anonymous texts probably came from one of the numerous Jewish schools of the Kabbalah that then existed in Europe, for the work is clearly inspired by the teachings of the Talmud and the Jewish faith. The *Clavicula* contains a collection of thirty-six pentacles (themselves symbols rich in magic and esoteric significance) which were intended to enable communication between the physical world and the different levels of the soul. There are various versions of the text, in numerous translations, and the content varies between them. However, most of the surviving texts date from the sixteenth and seventeenth centuries – although there is a Greek translation dating from the fifteenth.

In Tibet and India, the Buddhists and Hindus read this universal symbol of the hexagram in terms of the creator and his creation, while the Brahmins hold it to be the symbol of the god Vishnu. Originally, the two triangles were in green (upright triangle) and red (inverted triangle). Subsequently, these colours became black and white, the former representing the spirit, the latter the material world. For the Hindus, the upright triangle is associated with Shiva, Vishnu and Brahma (corresponding to the Christian God the Father, Son and Holy Ghost). The Son (Vishnu) can be seen to always occupy the middle position, being the intercessor between things divine and things earthly.

qara'im or *bnei mikra*: "he who follows the Scriptures". Karaism is a branch of Judaism that defends the sole authority of the Hebrew Scripture as the source of divine revelation, thus repudiating oral tradition.
**Menorah – the multibranched candelabra used in the rituals of Judaism. The arms of the seven-branched menorah, one of the oldest symbols of the Jewish faith, represent the seven archangels before the Throne of God: Michael, Gabriel, Samuel, Raphael, Zadkiel, Anael and Kassiel.

ALCHEMY AT THE PALACE OF SAXE-LAUENBURG

❼

Sasko-lauenburský (Rožmberský) dům
Hradčanské náměstí 10/62 (Hradčany Square)
• Closed to the public
• Tram: 22, Pražský hrad or Pohořelec stop

Rosenberg rivalry with the emperor

In addition to their work at the castle in the service of Rudolf II, the most skilled alchemists also worked for the Rosenberg family. This family of estate owners in southern Bohemia (Český Krumlov, Třeboň, Bechyně) also had property in Prague, such as the residence now known as the Palace of Saxe-Lauenburg in Hradčany Square. Alchemical experiments were

performed there too, Wilhelm von Rosenberg boasting that he spent more on alchemy than the emperor himself.

John Dee, Edward Kelley and the Czech Bavor Rodovský of Hustiřany, who all worked in Rudolf II's laboratories, were also in the Rosenbergs' service. It was Václav Lavín, author of the celebrated alchemist treatise *Pozemské nebe* (Earthly Paradise) and physician to Wilhelm von Rosenberg, who asked for the release of Bavor Rodovský, imprisoned in the castle's Black Tower.

The workplace of Wilhelm's brother Peter Vok von Rosenberg was also in the Palace of Saxe-Lauenburg (at the corner of Kanovnická Street).

TWO CZECH ALCHEMISTS

The presence of large numbers of foreign alchemists did not hinder the work of the many eminent Czech alchemists such as Šimon Tadeáš Budek,

the imperial inquisitor who had to investigate all those who came to Bohemia in search of precious stones and metals. He produced a vast alchemical collection of works in coded language, which is preserved at the Austrian National Library in Vienna.

Bavor Rodovský of Hustiřany also wrote several alchemical works, some of which are now in the Library of Prague's National Museum and the Voss Library at Leiden (Netherlands).

CHARLATAN ALCHEMIST LINE-UP

Many charlatans, drawn like moths to the flame, flocked to the imperial court in the hope of exploiting the emperor's weakness for rarities and miracles.

Thus one day a strange Greek known as Mamugna (Marco Bragadino) appeared, claiming to be an alchemist. Similarly, a travelling alchemist named Geronimo Alessandro Scotta demonstrated his powers in the presence of the emperor, who consulted him repeatedly on various astrological issues. In 1591, Philip Jacob Gustenhover, a Strasbourg goldsmith, is thought to have made several successful transmutations using a tincture supposedly purchased from the well-known adept Alexander Seton, the "Cosmopolite". Once the powder began to run out, however, he was forced to admit that he was unable to make it himself and he was imprisoned in the castle's White Tower. He fled to Strasbourg, where he was recaptured and taken back to Prague under escort.

Johann Heinrich Müller von Mühlenfels first practised his art in Swabia. Attracted by Rudolf II's fame, he arranged to shoot himself with a bullet made from lead amalgam, in order to prove his invulnerability, and also to carry out a transmutation of lead into gold in front of the emperor. However, to achieve this effect, he used a double-bottomed crucible in which he had previously hidden the gold!

A year after Rudolf's death, Hauser – another alchemist from the imperial court – was thrown into prison and tortured by order of Emperor Matthias when it was discovered that he wanted to use his occult arts against the monarch. He was expelled from the court and banished from Bohemia.

STANDARD OF THE PRAGUE CUBIT ❽

Hradčanská radnice (Town Hall)
Loretánská ulice 173
• Tram: 22, Pohořelec stop

*Traces
of an ancient
unit
of measurement*

At the entrance to the old Town Hall of Hradčany, built in the late 16th century (after which the district was declared an independent town), look for the metal strip running down the right side of the door.

This 591-millimetre strip has long served as a benchmark for the old measure of length in use in Prague: the cubit. It is divided into four sections, one of which is further divided into two.

Prague's cubit was introduced by King Přemysl Otakar I in 1228 as a unit of measurement: it was common at the time to take the length of a sovereign's body parts (foot, forearm, etc.) as standards for public use.

In case of dispute, or to supply the right length of fabric, for example, people could measure their merchandise accurately.

This use of the Prague cubit came to an end in January 1765, when Empress Maria Theresa ordered the Viennese cubit – the standard in Lower Austria – to be used instead.

Another Prague standard cubit can be found on the door of Novésto Mesto Town Hall in Charles Square (Karlovo náměstí) (see p. 95).

FRESCO OF ST BARBARA'S CHAPEL ❾

Loretánská ulice
• Tram: 22, Pohořelec stop

***Impalement
of a thief***

In Loretánská Street, the small chapel dedicated to St Barbara reflects a cruel legend relating to events of 1512: in that year, two knights convicted of theft were condemned to be impaled alive here. One of them managed to free himself and crawled to the Church of St Benedict.

The Czech Baroque painter V. V. Reiner probably depicted the legend in this chapel because St Barbara is the patron of those who die without receiving the last rites.

Inside the chapel, the small figure of an impaled convict can be seen in the background of the fresco.

LEGEND OF PRAGUE'S OLDEST CARILLON

The Loreta pilgrimage site possesses the oldest carillon in Prague. Composed of 30 bells cast by Amsterdam's master bell founder, Claudy Frémy, and assembled by Prague watchmaker Peter Neumann, the carillon rang out for the first time on 15 August 1695.

According to a local legend, the only possession of a poor widow with almost as many children as the number of bells was a purse full of coins. When the plague was raging through Prague, her children began to die. For each child that died, she gave a coin to the bellringer. When her last child died, she gave him her final coin. When she too fell ill and died, all the bells of Loreta chimed a beautiful melody.

HOME OF TYCHO BRAHE

At the entrance to the lane called Nový svět (New World), at No. 76, the old U zlatého noha (At the Golden Griffin) inn was for a while the home of the Danish astronomer–alchemist Tycho Brahe, who later settled with the emperor's consent in a house in the Pohořelec neighbourhood.

LEGEND OF THE CROSS IN LORETA SQUARE

Loretánské náměstí
• Tram: 22, Pohořelec stop

> **Back from the other side**

The so-called "Drahomíra's column" once stood in a corner of Loreta Square opposite a small cross that has come to be associated with the legend of the column, which was demolished by municipal decree in 1788.

According to this legend, the pagan princess Drahomíra (Dragomir) from a distant Slav tribe married the son of Ludmila (martyr and saint) of the Přemyslid dynasty, at the time of the evangelization of Bohemia that she had pioneered. It was said that Drahomíra used all her wiles to harm the Christians and was even allied with the Devil. One day, seeing her coachman (who had converted to Christianity) going into church to pray, she cursed the Christian faith at the top of her voice.

Since then, she is claimed to drive a chariot of fire that vanishes flaming into the abyss, one hour after midnight.

Others say that this is where the Devil took the countess of Černín Palace, according to another local legend (see below), and carried her off underground as penance, forcing her to wear shoes made from bread dough.

LEGEND OF ČERNÍN PALACE

The legend goes that the architect Francesco Caratti built the palace of Count Černín, the largest in Bohemia (150 m long), without a written contract. The count died before the palace was completed and his widow failed to honour her husband's debt. The aggrieved architect turned to the deceased's brother, who belonged to a Prague secret society and promised to help him. The architect was blindfolded and taken outside the city walls, where masked members of this society contacted the count's ghost. The apparition was forced to sign a contract and the architect was finally paid.

CANNONBALLS AT THE CHURCH OF OUR LADY OF THE ANGELS

Loretánské náměstí (Loreta Square)
- Church open for Mass: Monday to Friday, 6pm; Sunday 8.30am
- Crèche during Christmas festivities
- Tram: 22, 25, 27, Pohořelec stop

O ver 50 cannonballs can still be seen embedded in the façade of the Church of Our Lady of the Angels (Panny Marie Andělské).

Memories of a bombardment

These are vestiges of the Prussian artillery's bombardment of Prague in 1757. During the Seven Years' War (1756–63), Prussian troops led by Emperor Frederick II invaded Bohemia and fought many bloody battles with the Austrian troops. After the 1757 Battle of Štěrboholy, the Prussian army besieged Prague, occupying Břevnov Monastery and Hvězda Park in Bílá Hora and pillaging the castle district.

The church in Loreta Square belongs to the oldest Capuchin monastery in Bohemia, built between 1600 and 1601. The monastery is interconnected with the Loreta via a roofed passageway.

More cannonballs from the same era are embedded in the wall of the Church of St Karel Veliký at Karlov (see p. 105).

UNIQUE CRÈCHE
The Church of Our Lady of the Angels is famous for its crèche, dating from 1780. Designed by a monk familiar with the tradition of the Neapolitan nativity scene, it is unique in the Czech Republic with its 48 almost life-size figures (32 human and 16 animal). The largest are the shepherds, the tallest of whom stands at 175 centimetres.

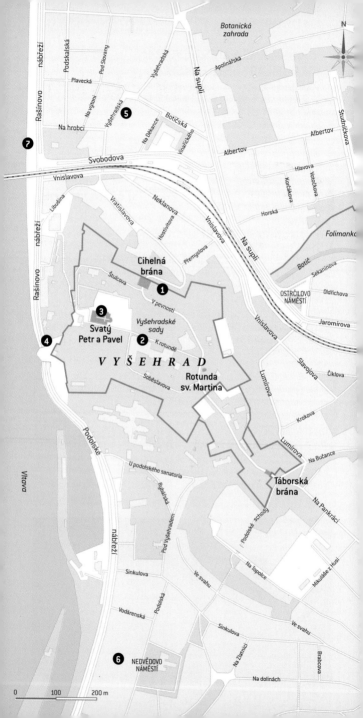

Botanická zahrada

N

náměstí

Rašínovo

Podskalská
Plavecká
Pod Slovany
Vyšehradská

Na výtoni
Vyšehradská
Na hrobci
5
Na Děkance
Vratislavce

Vyšehradská

Na slupi

Apolinářská

Botičská

Albertov

Studničkova

Albertov

Hlavova
Votočkova
Kateřinská

Horská

7

Svobodova

Vnislavova

náměstí

Rašínovo

Neklanova
Vratislavova
Hostivítova
Přemyslova
Vnislavova

Na slupi

Folimanka

Libušina

Botič
Sekaninova
Oldřichova

OSTRČILOVO
NÁMĚSTÍ

Jaromírova

Cihelná
brána
1

Štulcova

V pevnosti

3
Svatý
Petr a Pavel

4

Vyšehradské
sady
2
K rotundě

V Y Š E H R A D

Soběslavova

Rotunda
sv. Martina

Vnislavova

Lumírova

Stavojova

Čiklova

Krokova

Lumírova
Na Bučance

Táborská
brána

Na Pankráci

Podolské

U podolského sanatoria
Rodašská

Pod Vyšehradem

Podolské schody

Na Topolce

Na Topolce

Mikuláše z Husi

Vltava

náměstí

Sinkulova
Podolská
Vodárenská

Ve svahu

Sinkulova

Na zlatnici

Ve svahu

Brabcova

6
NEDVĚDOVO
NÁMĚSTÍ

Na dolinách

0   100   200 m

VYŠEHRAD

LEGENDS OF THE GORLICE CASEMATES

Pevnost Vyšehrad
• Open daily, 1 April-31 Oct, 9.30am-6pm, 1 Nov-31 March, 9.30am-5pm
• Metro: Vyšehrad; Tram: 3, 7, 17, 21, Výtoň stop

*Myths
of the secret
underground
galleries*

On the northern side of Vyšehrad fortress is the entrance to a system of vaulted tunnels. The largest of these (330 square metres, height 13 metres) is known as Gorlice Hall and is now a lapidarium.

It is claimed that the tunnels excavated in Vyšehrad hill date back to the reign of Princess Libuše. Some are thought to have served as shelters in times of danger, others to horde treasure. The fabulous treasure of Libuše herself is thought to be kept there, guarded by a lion. Access is said to be possible only at midnight on Good Friday, when the ground opens up for a few moments.

At a place called Na jezerce (At the Little Lake), a spring still runs today. This is the site of Libuše's Bath. A subterranean passage is supposed to lead there from Vyšehrad fortress, accessible even during troubled times.

The Vyšehrad rocks also conceal a sleeping army, mustered by Princess Libuše herself, which will emerge whenever Bohemia is in great turmoil.

While Vyšehrad was being fortified during the second half of the 17th century, this vast network of tunnels, some of which are now open to the public, was built for defensive purposes.

Gorlice is a town in present-day Poland. A major battle in which many Czech soldiers fought took place there during the First World War. The town was so named to commemorate the underground galleries of Vyšehrad.

MYSTICISM AT VYŠEHRAD

The majestic mass of Vyšehrad stands on the opposite bank of the Vltava upstream from Prague Castle. Its role in early history is still shrouded in mystery. Some people argue that the fortress was not founded until the 10th century, later than the castle. The legendary version is as rich as the historical documentation is sparse – it teems with colourful detail about the life and doings of the Czech sibyl, the legendary Princess Libuše and her husband, Prince Přemysl the ploughman, founder of the ruling dynasty. This apparent wealth of information is rather suspect, however, and bears out the backdrop of legend, reaching back to before the Slavs, Celts or perhaps even earlier times. Heroes and kings are incarnations of the gods and take their place in the eternal cycle of Nature.

Libuše, identified with the pagan goddess of spring (Venus or Freya), is purified during her ritual ablutions in the baths at Vyšehrad to encourage the first appearance of the fertilising force.

Přemysl the labourer, corresponding to the fecund god of heat and light who comes from the North, ploughs his furrow in the sacred field and bonds with his companion.

Also shut up in the cliff is a horse and more of Libuše's treasure trove: a golden frog and a hen with 12 golden eggs.

In the gloomy forest near the Botič stream, Bivoj (Hercules) hunts wild boar with his superhuman strength, while the band of Bohemian Amazons sharpen their arrows.

Seven legendary former princes of Vyšehrad correspond to the names of the days of the week and the seven planets known at the time, succeeding one another in the exercise of power. Legend tells of conflicts over the mining of various metals during their reigns. The names of the old planetary gods of metal reverberate in the list learned by Czech schoolchildren:

Nezamysl, Mnata, Voien, Vnislav, Křesomysl, Neklan, Hostivít (*Mnata*, for example, is associated with the Moon, *Voien* with Mars, *Křesomysl* with Jupiter, and so on).

So Vyšehrad, in the context of Prague, mirrors the cosmos and chaos through the web of analogies that has formed around it: from Monday to Sunday, from Vyšehrad to Hrad (the castle), from Moon to Sun, from Charles to Rudolf, from silver to gold ...

VYŠEHRAD'S GHOSTS

Pevnost Vyšehrad, Rotunda Sv Martina
Metro: Vyšehrad; Tram: 3, 7, 17, 21, Výtoň stop

Vyšehrad is particularly renowned for its spectres, as numerous as those that haunt the city itself.

According to legend, at night the ghost of a dog attached to a red-hot iron chain runs from the Rotunda of St Martin to the fortress gate. Another dog, headless and on fire, appears next to a chariot from Hell, with a headless coachman driving headless horses. This apparition haunts the walls of Vyšehrad.

Likewise, the ghosts of soldiers and nuns sometimes wander around; and from the small Romanesque bridge near the church, the pounding of horses' hooves can be heard.

The headless ghost of the White Lady appears near the small vaulted passage known as Myší tell (Mousehole). She is alleged to take that path out of the depths of the rock, where she watches over treasures in a cave guarded by a dog with eyes of fire. A curse hangs over the White Lady: it will be lifted the day that the buried treasure is discovered. Only then will the ghost be reunited with her head and find release from the evil spell.

On the rocky slopes below Vyšehrad, the ruins of a medieval stronghold known as Libušina lázeň (Libuše's Bath) can still be seen today. The White Lady, who might be the ghost of Libuše, also appears here. When the moon shines through an opening in the ruins, it is said that the White Lady is at the window. Those who lived at the foot of the cliff used to take this as an ill omen that heralded an imminent drowning.

In the Church of Sts Peter & Paul another ghost, the "Lady of Hannewald", sometimes appears during Mass, emerging from the Hannewald chapel.

A bottomless pit is also said to lie within Vyšehrad rock. It was formed during the Hussite wars when the coffin containing the relics of Longinus (the soldier whose spear pierced the side of Christ), previously sent back to Rome by Charles IV, was thrown over the cliff: Longinus' body and spear slid out of the coffin and plunged into the water without touching the bottom,

while the sarcophagus floated on the surface. The coffin is now on display in the church, serving as a base for the altar.

COLUMN OF ZARDAN THE DEVIL

Pevnost Vyšehrad, kostel Sv Petra a Pavla (Church of Sts Peter & Paul)
• Metro: Vyšehrad; Tram: 3, 7, 17, 21, Výtoň stop

Exorcism in Prague

In Vyšehrad park, at the side entrance to the cemetery, lie the three pieces of a broken column, perhaps the most famous "*corpus delicti*" for which we can blame the Devil, as the pieces are also recorded in dictionaries of demonology.*

According to tradition, St Peter commanded the Devil to bring the stones needed to build the new church at Vyšehrad. The place was run by a priest who had resorted to diabolical powers and descended to Hell before he repented. Peter took pity on him and advised him to wager that he would have time to finish celebrating Mass before the Devil could bring back a column from St Peter's Basilica in Rome. The Devil would have succeeded had St Peter not made him fall, three times, near Venice (which is why, they say, the column is broken into three pieces).

During his flight from Rome back to Prague, the Devil left an engraved stone with visible traces of his claws and image near the village of Kolence in southern Bohemia.

However, arriving too late in Prague and so having lost his bet, he threw the column onto the Vyšehrad rocks in a rage.

In 1655, during an exorcism, the Devil proclaimed his name as Zardan through the mouth of the possessed. Since then, the column has borne that name.

Note that some histories of demonology mention a certain Václav Králíček, a former priest of Vyšehrad Church, as a famous exorcist.

A MENHIR AT VYŠEHRAD?

The Devil's column is sometimes thought to be an ancient menhir. The work of a 9th-century Bavarian geographer already records that a stone pillar was standing at Petřín in the year 750. Bishop Adalbert of Prague thought this column was a pagan symbol and ordered that it should be moved to Vyšehrad. During the journey it split into three pieces, which are still lying there …

Not far from the Devil's column, opposite the Church of Sts Peter & Paul, is a stone wall thought to weigh more than the largest section of the column. Its origin, purpose and builders are unknown. It may have been a menhir of which only the lower section has been preserved, used during the Christian era as a base for a cross or statue.

*J. Tondriau and R. Villeneuve, *Dictionnaire du diable et de la démonologie*, 1968, p. 46.

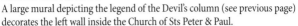

NEARBY

THE FRESCO OF THE DEVIL
Church of Sts Peter & Paul

③

A large mural depicting the legend of the Devil's column (see previous page) decorates the left wall inside the Church of Sts Peter & Paul.

It shows the Devil's three actions simultaneously as if it were a medieval comic strip: on the horizon, we first see the Devil rushing from Rome to Prague; then above the church, the Devil with a column as it was broken by St Peter; and finally, inside the church, a broken column with a priest standing on it.

According to some reports, the Zardan column originally lay inside Sts Peter & Paul, below a ragged hole in the ceiling.

THE LEGENDARY HORSE ŠEMÍK: AN ARCHETYPE OF THE "SPOKEN CABAL"?

The words horse and mare occur often in alchemist terminology. They recall the Latin word cabalus and "cabal" as the hidden speech of Nature; the German word for Šemík is *schamig*, meaning "hidden".

If the cabal had a hidden discourse, then Šemík's surreal jump could be identified with the art of alchemy at its highest level.

Hermetism also distinguishes between the "spoken cabal" based on assonance, also called the "language of birds", and the Jewish Kabbalah in which there is an intimate relationship between numbers and letters. Such a distinction is found in the written forms of the word cabal: with one b when referring to the "spoken cabal" and two to refer to the Jewish Kabbalah.

And Šemík speaks! This mythical theme not only recalls the "spoken cabal" but also the universal discourse of Nature and its creatures.

When Šemík whispered in Horymír's ear: "Hold on tight, master," the hidden meaning of his leap should not be overlooked.

According to another legend, Šemík was from a special bloodline of white horses* from the village of Koněpruské west of Prague, the former Celtic stronghold of Bohemia. Note that the name Koněpruské (Koněprusý) also hints at the "spoken cabal" because *kůň* (plural *koně*) means "horse(s)" and *prusý* means "blond."

Although this legend is thought to be comparatively recent, analysis of the names and comparison with other myths link it to the archetypal Vyšehrad epic cycle. To cite just one example, etymologically, Horymír (Montanus) is he "who measures the mountain" or "who brings peace". But Montanus (Bergmann, "mountain man" or "miner" in German mythology) also means "cobold", the spirit of the mine who prevents uncontrolled prospecting and tries to reconcile miners with the order of Nature.

In this mythological hierarchy, Prince Křesomysl is the representation of Wotan or Odin (identified with Jupiter), "who needs precious metals".

Šemík (i.e. discreet, hidden, obscure), for his part, is none other than the white Sun-horse of Přemysl, the mythical founder of the kingdom of Bohemia.

WHERE IS ŠEMÍK'S TOMB?

The village of Neumětely, about 40 kilometres south-west of Prague, was the domain of the horseman Horymír. North of the village is Košík (Basket) hill where, according to legend, a castle was built. After his famous leap over the ramparts of Vyšehrad and the Vltava, he was buried outside the walls of Neumětely. The careful upkeep of the tomb of the legendary horse shows the tenacity of the legend.

Šemík's tomb, in undressed stone, is at the centre of an open space covered with a tiled roof. In the 19th century the stone was moved and the grave opened, but nothing was found.

The people of Neumětely, respectful of tradition, demanded that the tomb be restored to its original state.

*Plavý (blond) in its old sense means white, so plavý kůň translates as white horse.

LIBUŠE'S BATH

Pevnost, kostel Sv Petra a Pavla (Church of Sts Peter & Paul)
• Metro: Vyšehrad; Tram: 3, 7, 17, 21, Výtoň stop

Horymír's legendary leap

Libuše's Bath, by the ruins of a small watchtower below the Vyšehrad ramparts, is according to legend the place where Princess Libuše bathed.

This is the same place over which Horymír jumped on his horse Šemík: at the time of Prince Křesomysl, whose seat was at Vyšehrad, the horseman Horymír was sentenced to death for attempting to stop the extraction of silver at the mining town of Příbram, south of Prague. Legend says that he was saved thanks to a phenomenal leap by Šemík, his faithful talking horse, who cleared the ramparts and crags overlooking the Vltava.

After carrying Horymír to his home village of Neumětely (south-west of Prague), the injured and exhausted horse died.

This old Prague legend is often claimed to be inspired by foreign myths like those of Dietrich von Bern or Theodoric the Great, which also feature a horse like Šemík.

MERMAN SCULPTURE

U Tunglů house
Vyšehradská ulice 8
• Tram: 3, 7, 17, 21, Výtoň stop

The mysterious house called U Tunglů on Vyšehradská Street features a striking statue that looks rather like a monkey.

The water sprite of Podskalí

The statue is in fact a water sprite (merman), illustrating a common legend in Podskalí, a village that is strongly connected to the waters of the Vltava.

According to this legend, the merman of Podskalí (almost every village in the Czech Republic has its own water sprite) once drowned the son of a fisherman. In retaliation, the boy's mother continued to take out her revenge on the merman's children until he promised to stop luring the children of Podskalí to their deaths.

Another story about this house claims that it was haunted for a while by a headless monk.

Today, Vyšehradská Street follows the old road that connected Vyšehrad to the Old Town, before the development of the New Town.

WHAT IS A MERMAN?

The water sprite or merman (masculine of "mermaid", *wasserman* in German, *hastrman* or *vodník* in Czech) is a fabled being in Czech and German folktales who lives under water where he keeps the souls of the drowned hidden in little pots. With his green skin, large eyes and webbed fingers, he looks distinctly like a toad. One day this creature haunting the lakes captured a young woman, shut her up in his palace under the water and got her with child. She wished to return to the land for a single day and promised to return. The merman agreed, but when the young woman broke her promise he went to fetch her at the home of her mother, who refused to give up her daughter. In his anger, he whipped up a storm that dumped the body of their child on his wife's doorstep.

Czech composer Antonín Dvořák, noted for turning folklore into romantic music, based his 1896 opera *Rusalka* on this tale.

PRAGUE WATER TREATMENT MUSEUM

Podolská 15/17
• Tel: 272 172 345
• www.pvk.cz/muzeum-prazskeho-vodarenstvi.html
• jiri.dejmek@pvk.cz
• Museum visits by reservation only
• Tram: 3, 16, 17, 21, Podolská vodárna stop

The Water Palace

Built of reinforced concrete between 1927 and 1929, the water treatment plant known as the Water Palace is among Prague's most beautiful industrial heritage sites and one of a series of remarkable buildings designed by the architect Antonín Engel (1878–1958).

In the early 1950s, a second filtering system was installed on the south side, following the architect's original plans and linked to the first building by a bridge.

The recently modernised plant is still in operation. It draws water from the Vltava and complements the supply of drinking water to the city, which also uses water from the sources of the Káraný and Želivka.

Since 1952, the Prague Water Treatment Museum (Muzeum pražského vodárenství) has been open on the factory premises, allowing the public to visit the old filtering stations.

The inside of the plant is fitted with glass dividing walls that offer stunning views of the working spaces.

In the museum you can see ancient wooden pipes from the time of Rudolf II, as well as old water pumps.

NEARBY

WATER-LEVEL GAUGE ON THE VLTAVA AT VÝTOŇ

Rašínovo nábřeží (Rašín embankment)
• Tram: 3, 7, 17, 21, Výtoň stop

Any rise in the water level that might lead to flooding is monitored by a number of gauges throughout the city. Although the oldest is probably the stone head of Bradáč (the Bearded Man) on the embankment next to Charles Bridge (see p. 71), another gauge can be seen on the banks of the Vltava at Výtoň: the depth of the water is monitored on dials set into a small stone tower on the quayside.

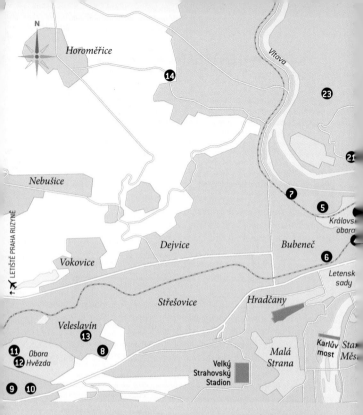

OUTSIDE THE CENTRE - NORTH

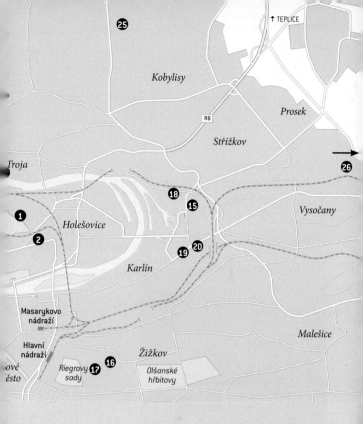

↑ TEPLICE

Kobylisy

Prosek

Střížkov

R8

Troja

Vysočany

Holešovice

Karlín

Masarykovo nádraží

Hlavní nádraží

Malešice

Žižkov

Riegrovy sady

Olšanské hřbitovy

…ové …ěsto

MAROLD'S PANORAMA ❶

Výstaviště
- Tel: 220 103 210
- Open Tuesday to Friday 1pm–5pm; Saturday and Sunday 10am–5pm; closed in winter
- Metro: Holešovické nádraží; Tram: 5, 12, 14, 15, 17, Výstaviště stop

> *Panorama of a memorable battle*

At Výstaviště the Maroldovo panorama (Marold's Panorama) is an astounding circular building constructed in 1908 to the plans of Jan Koula.

Its interior walls are decorated with the remarkable work of Czech painter Luděk Marold, *The Battle of Lipany*, painted in 1897–98 in collaboration with Václav Jansa. The artefacts relating to the battle placed in front of the painting were installed by Karel Štapfer and other artists.

At 11 metres high and 95 metres long, and with a surface area of 1,045 square metres, Marold's Panorama is by far the largest illustration of a Bohemian historical event.

WHAT IS A PANORAMA?

The panorama, which had its heyday in the 19th century, is a rotunda lit from above in which a mural painted in trompe l'œil is installed on the circular interior walls. There are still about a dozen panoramas around the world. Here are some of them:

Mesdag Panorama in The Hague (Netherlands). The oldest panorama in the world to be preserved at its original site.

Racławice Panorama (Wrocław, Poland)

Bourbaki Panorama (Lucerne, Switzerland)

Panorama of Our Lady of Lourdes (France)

Thun Panorama (Switzerland)

Panorama of the Battle of Murten (Switzerland)

Pleven Panorama (Bulgaria)

Panorama of the Battle of Waterloo (Belgium)

In Brussels, a former panorama has been turned into a parking lot (see *Secret Brussels* in this series of guidebooks).

ENTRANCE TO CROSS CLUB

Plynární 1096/23, Praha 7
• Metro: Holešovické nádraží

Not far from Holešovice metro station, an extraordinary metallic sculpture forms the entrance to a multicultural venue that includes a café, a small cinema, galleries and live music.

A futuristic club

The Cross Club is a spectacle in itself. Its mesmerising futuristic industrial motif is by set designer František S. Chmelik.

RUDOLF'S ADIT

③

Stromovka
Gate near Šlechta restaurant
• Tel: 777 293 339 • www.nautilus.cz
• Closed to the public
• Metro: Holešovické nádraží; Tram: 5, 12, 14, 15, 17, Výstaviště stop

> *A masterpiece of engineering*

The royal park (popularly called Stromovka) of some 90 hectares is one of the most remarkable public spaces in Prague. It was developed in the 16th century during the reign of Rudolf II, who wanted to rebuild a hunting lodge on the heights and enlarge the ponds in order to raise trout and game birds. As the waters of the Vltava supplied the large pond at Stromovka, an extraordinary gallery called Rudolfová štola (Rudolf's Adit – i.e. entrance to an underground passage) was cut through Letná hill.

Lazarus Ercker von Schreckenfels, the kingdom's Chief Inspector of Mines who was responsible for the project, had the inspired idea of using the gradient of the slope of the Vltava between the Old Town and Stromovka to let water flow into the park. After 10 years of work, the inauguration of Rudolfová štola took place on 17 July 1593.

The gallery, with a difference between the upper and lower levels of 110 cm, a height of 2–4 m and a width of 90–150 cm, is 1,098 m long. It ends in Stromovka Park at a gate surmounted by a carved crown with Rudolf's initial and the date marking the end of construction (1593).

A small building, the "havírna", on the left bank above the stone dam of Helmovský jez, draws water from the river to feed the ponds of the royal park.

VENTILATION DUCTS OF RUDOLF'S ADIT

Originally there were five of these ducts, two of which can still be seen.
One of these is in the middle of the road near the intersection of Čechova and Sládkova streets in the Letná neighbourhood. With a depth of 43 metres, it is topped with a cast-iron cowl.
The aerial section of the duct that can be seen at No. 16 Čechova comes from a side passage off the main gallery.
Another air duct 42 metres deep can be seen at the junction of Kostelní and Nad štolou streets at the exit leading to the tennis courts.

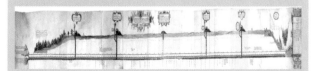

1: entrance to the gallery
2–3: ventilation ducts
4: gallery exit at Stromovka

SUNDIAL AT THE GOVERNOR'S SUMMER RESIDENCE ❹

Stromovka 56
• Tram: 1, 8, 15, 25, 26, Letenské náměstí stop; Bus: 131, Sibirske náměstí stop

A distinctive sundial

In a corner of the small garden of Místodržitelský letohrádek (Governor's summer residence), on the southern slopes of Stromovka Park, is a remarkable spherical sundial with a movable indicator. Dating back to 1698, it was restored in 1772.

Engraved on the red marble surface are Latin inscriptions and signs of

the zodiac, the Sun, Moon and planets.

The Governor's summer residence, built in the 13th century, has stood in its current form since the 19th century. The Luxembourg, Jagiellon and Habsburg dynasties used it as a hunting lodge. During the Thirty Years' War it was the temporary headquarters of Wittenberg, Commander-in-Chief of the Swedish forces, which is why it was not destroyed like many of the city's palaces.

In 1804, the royal park was opened to the public and in the same year the restoration of the residence in neo-Gothic style was begun. The building's name derives from its use as a summer seat of the royal government in the 19th century.

Only one section of the spiral staircase is preserved in its original form. At the top of the steps is a stone lion bearing the monogram of Czech King Vladislav Jagiello (W) as part of a coat of arms surmounting a column.

EMPEROR'S MILL CAVE

Mlýnská ulice 22, Praha 6
• Tel: 720 141 462
• www.cisarskymlyn.com
• The cave can be seen through an iron gate
• Bus: 131, Nemocnice Bubeneč stop; Train: Nádraží Bubeneč stop

Is this where Rudolf II meditated?

The only vestige of the old mill in the royal domain of Bubeneč (Císařský mlýn residence), built from 1581 and acquired by Rudolf II in 1584, is the cave with a gate surmounted by the initial R, surrounded by residential homes.

This man-made cave was probably the emperor's private meditation chapel.

The Emperor's Mill was also used for cutting precious stones – in Rudolf II's time, this was the task of the celebrated Dionysios Miseroni, and later of his son.

THE BEAUTIFUL VILLAS ON SLAVÍČKOVA STREET

❻

Slavíčkova ulice, Bubeneč
• Metro: Hradčanská; Tram: 15, 36, Špejchar stop

Artists' enclave

Slavíčkova's association with artists goes back a long way: although the street is named after the celebrated Czech Impressionist painter Antonín Slavíček, until 1947 it was known as Mánesova (Josef Mánes was the 19th-century Czech Revivalist who painted the original calendar wheel for the Astronomical Clock in the Old Town), then, for a short period after the Second World War, as Mařákova (after the landscape artist Julius Mařák).

Some of the houses are resounding architectural triumphs.

The villa at No. 17 was the home of architect Jan Koula – he built it in 1895 and 1896 in a style combining folk architecture and late Gothic, and was also responsible for the *sgraffiti* on the façade. A statue of the hermit St Ivan, sculpted by his neighbour Stanislav Sucharda, stands in a recess to the right of the entrance.

The villa next door, No. 15, was built in 1896 for Stanislav Sucharda before his brother, the sculptor Vojtěch Sucharda, bought it. On the façade is a mural

by Czech painter Mikoláš Aleš depicting Božetěch, abbot of the Benedictine monastery on the Sázava River, the first sculptor whose work is recorded in Bohemia.

Opposite, at No. 7, the villa of the painter and Art Nouveau architect K. V. Mašek resembles the home of Jan Koula but with even richer decoration. In the garden, a lovely terrace leads to an artificial cave.

Finally, the villa at No. 4 was built in 1907 by eminent architect Dušan Jurkovič.

FORMER WASTEWATER TREATMENT PLANT ❼

Papírenská 6, Bubeneč
• Tel: 602 318 357 • www.staracistirna.cz • infocistirna@gmail.com
• Open daily all year round
• Tours at 11am and 2pm on weekdays and 10am, 12 noon, 2pm and 4pm at weekends
• Bus: 131, Nádraží Bubeneč stop

An industrial monument

The former wastewater treatment plant at Bubeneč, classified as a historic monument, is a major achievement of Czech industrial architecture.

The buildings have been restored since 1991 and you can now visit this spectacular place with its underground pipes and steam-powered machine room, finding out about the history of sewers and wastewater treatment.

Built between 1901 and 1906 to plans by the British engineer W. H. Lindley, the station was in use until 1967, when a modern water treatment plant was built nearby on the island of Císařský ostrov.

FRESCO OF SAINT GUNTHER'S MIRACLE ❽

Břevnov Monastery
Markétská 28/1, Břevnov
• Tel: 220 406 270 • klaster@brevnov.cz
• Guided tours Saturday and Sunday at 10am, 2pm, 4pm;
Monday–Friday by appointment

The peacock's bent wing

The ceiling of the Tereziánský room, on the first floor of the Břevnov Monastery, was created by the Bavarian fresco painter and architect Cosmas Damian Asam in 1729.

In one corner he shows the miracle of the Blessed Gunther (Zázrak blahoslaveného Vintíře), in one of the best-preserved and most prized frescoes of Baroque Prague.

The fresco depicts an incredible legend in which the saint of Šumava Vintíř mountain (Gunther) attended a feast at which roast peacock was served.

As this feast was being held on a day of fasting, the saint, noticing the sacrilege, caused the roasted bird to fly off the table.

A careful look at the fresco reveals a curious detail: the right wing of the peacock in flight is back to front – a physically impossible feat …

Legend also has it that Abbot Othmar Zinke, who commissioned the fresco, would not pay the sum owed to the artist, who might have been seeking revenge by depicting the peacock in this way.

MONUMENT TO THE BATTLE OF BÍLÁ HORA ❾

Ruzyně
Řepská or Pod mohylou streets
• Tram: 22, Bílá Hora stop; Bus: 164, 225

Souvenir of White Mountain

At Bílá Hora (White Mountain) on 8 November 1620 the final phase of the first major battle of the Thirty Years' War took place, the political and military consequences of which deeply marked Bohemia and the whole of Europe.

The battle was short but bloody: although the Moravian foot soldiers put up strong resistance, they finally had to take refuge behind the walls of the Hvězda summer residence, where they were massacred. The then King of Bohemia Frederick I (Czech: Fridrich Falcký), nicknamed the Winter King for his short reign, hastily abandoned Prague and the Catholic League celebrated victory over the Bohemian Estates, which had lost 2,000 men.

A monument by the sculptor Frantisek Bílek was erected in 1920 on the highest point of Bílá Hora plain to commemorate the 300th anniversary of one of the most important battles on Czech lands.

DESCARTES: SOLDIER–PHILOSOPHER

During the Battle of Bílá Hora, the eminent French philosopher René Descartes is said to have fought in the emperor's army as a lookout in the artillery.

There is a legend that he was wounded and, on regaining consciousness, he uttered the famous words: *"Dubito ergo cogito; cogito ergo sum"* (I doubt, therefore I think; I think, therefore I am).

ENGRAVING OF THE *ADORATION OF CHRIST* **⑩**

Chapel of Our Lady Victorious
Zbečenská, Ruzyně
• Tours by appointment with the Břevnov Monastery
• Tram: 22, Bílá Hora stop; Bus: 164, 225

A picture that led to victory at White Mountain

At the outbreak of the Thirty Years' War (1618–48), the Carmelite monk Dominic, armed with his blessed sword, left Rome to fight with the Catholic forces. He accompanied the Bavarian army of Duke Maximilian I as far as Bohemia. Besides the sword, he had with him an engraving of the *Adoration of Christ* found at Strakonice Castle (although another version of the story claims that the image comes from Štěnovice chapel in south-west Bohemia), which had been vandalized by the Protestants: the eyes of all the figures,

with the exception of the Baby Jesus, had been put out. After blessing the Catholic soldiers with this picture hanging round his neck, he prayed for them throughout the course of the Battle of Bílá Hora, so he and his miraculous picture were given credit for the victory.

Only later did the battle begin to be described as a theatre of supernatural events: shots had allegedly bounced off the picture, and lightning is said to have blinded Protestant soldiers. After the battle, Brother Dominic carried the engraving to Rome and handed it over to Pope Gregory XV.

In 1622, the engraving was solemnly moved from the Roman Basilica of Santa Maria Maggiore to the Church of the Conversion of St Paul, which was renamed Santa Maria della Vittoria for the occasion.

Although the altar where the engraving was kept was destroyed by a fire in 1833, there are still three copies of which two are from that period. One can be seen in Rome in the sacristy of Santa Maria della Vittoria, and another in the Church of Our Lady Victorious (kostel Panny Marie Vítězné) in Malá Strana. The third and later engraving (1708) is in the chapel dedicated to Our Lady Victorious, which replaced a small chapel to St Wenceslas erected on the site of the battle.

The impressive dome of the chapel was probably built by G. Santini, and the paintings executed by C. D. Asam, J. A. Schöpf and W. L. Reiner.

The legend of the magical power of the engraving is also the theme of a relief above the main door of the chapel.

ESOTERIC STUCCOS
OF STAR SUMMER PALACE

⑪

Liboc
• Tram: 22, 1, Vypich stop; Bus: 179, 184, 191, 510, Petřiny stop

A true philosopher's dwelling?

Archduke Ferdinand of Tyrol himself is thought to have put forward the plans for Letohrádek hvězda (Star Summer Palace) in the form of a magical hexagon, to carry on his clandestine affair with his mistress Philipina Welser. Construction of the villa started in 1555, with three floors and a cellar, the figures of the date expressing not only the number of rooms per floor (one room on the top floor, and five on the others) but the four alchemical elements from highest to lowest: fire, air, water and earth.

Close to the site of the tragic Battle of White Mountain, the Star Summer Palace was raided in the 18th century before being used as a powder store and finally opened to the public in the mid-19th century.

Despite this chequered history, the villa managed to preserve its beautiful ground-floor stuccos, inspired by ancient Roman designs, each corresponding to a god of the Roman pantheon associated with the planets and the metals, as found in the tracts of the early alchemists.

The circular central hall, representing the Sun (Gold), has at its centre a relief of the legendary father of the Roman nation, Aeneas, bearing his father and his family's household gods to safety as Troy burns. This hero with his solar characteristics sailed westwards, taking his bearings from the Evening Star, before founding Rome. In the Star villa, it is also significant that this relief shows Aeneas pointing in the same direction as that in which we see Venus (the Evening Star) rising, through the window of the west corridor.

On the vault of the central hall, six reliefs depict the legendary history of Rome in an iconographic group called *Speculum Virtutis* (Mirror of the Virtues): they share the themes often taken up by alchemists. In the relief representing familial love, for example, we find the legend of old Cimon and his daughter Pero, who visited him in prison and offered him her breast, a motif reminiscent of the common alchemist injunction, "Give the old man the Virgin's milk to drink."

STAR SUMMER PALACE AS END POINT ON THE ESOTERIC ROYAL WAY

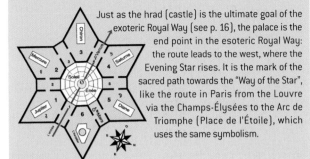

Just as the hrad (castle) is the ultimate goal of the exoteric Royal Way (see p. 16), the palace is the end point in the esoteric Royal Way: the route leads to the west, where the Evening Star rises. It is the mark of the sacred path towards the "Way of the Star", like the route in Paris from the Louvre via the Champs-Élysées to the Arc de Triomphe (Place de l'Étoile), which uses the same symbolism.

NEARBY

STONE OF THE POET ANDRÉ BRETON   (12)

Inspired poets have always been close to the works of the ancient alchemists. With great perspicacity, the French surrealist poet André Breton, during his stay in Prague in 1935, captures all the deep esoteric poetic value of the Star Summer Palace that he transcribed in the magical ending of a chapter of his novel *L'Amour Fou* (Mad Love): "Overhanging the abyss, in the shape of the philosopher's stone, the star-shaped castle spreads out." His famous friend Max Ernst illustrated this text with a sketch of the imaginary star.

In 2005, the 450th anniversary of the foundation of the Star Summer Palace, an exhibition was devoted to the stars as well as their influence and inspiration on the building. On this occasion, a stone engraved with a fragment of this extract from Breton's writing in the two languages and bearing his signature was installed next to the villa (left of main entrance).

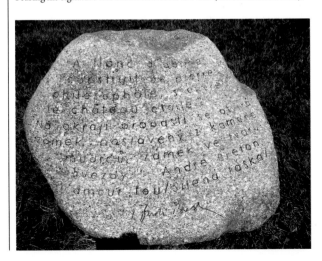

VĚTRNÍK GUESTHOUSE

U Větrníku 40/1
Praha 6
• Tel: 220 612 404 or 220 513 390 • pension@vetrnik1722.cz

**The last
windmill**

In the Petřiny district the Větrník (Windmill) guesthouse is a surprise, with its round tower attached to the main building.

This is the last vestige of the Dutch type of windmill in Prague.

It was in 1277 that Godefrid, Abbot of Břevnov, ordered the construction of a wooden windmill for the monastery. The mill had its own wells, 30 metres deep, which are still used today.

Rebuilt in stone in 1772, it was purchased from the monastery in 1794 by the family of miller Kohoutek and produced wheat flour into the 1860s. In 1905 it was converted and became part of a residential site. It is now a guesthouse.

HOUSLE SPRING ⑭

Lysolaje
Nad Pramenem
• Bus: 160, 355, Lysolaje stop

*Miraculous
therapeutic
waters*

Lysolaje was a small farming community and vineyard that once belonged to Prague Castle.

Extensive archaeological digs have revealed the existence of dwellings since prehistoric times. Since 1999 the site, known as Praha–Lysolaje, has been incorporated into the city of Prague while keeping its rural and romantic aspect.

At the foot of a deep wooded ravine, west of Lysolaje, is a spring called Housle (Violin), which once supplied drinking water for the community. Local tradition attests to the therapeutic qualities of this water, thought to be miraculous.

Just above the spring, an imitation Baroque chapel was built in 1863. Inside is a painting of the Seven Sorrows of the Blessed Virgin Mary.

TRIBUTE TO BOHUMIL HRABAL

Na Hrázi, Libeň
• Metro: Palmovka; Tram: 10, 24, 25, 3, 8, 12, 15, 19, 24, Palmovka stop

On the Barrier of Eternity

At 24/326 Na Hrázi (The Barrier), poetically named "On the Barrier of Eternity" in Palmovka, Bohumil Hrabal, one of the greatest Czech writers of the 20th century, lived in a small house for 23 years from 1950. This was one of the happiest periods of his life, and the old Libeň neighbourhood is the setting for several of his books.

The massive clean-up of this strange district culminated in 1988 with the construction of the Palmovka metro and bus station. The writer's home and some other houses on Na Hrázi were demolished and replaced by a monstrous concrete wall.

In 2000, the artist T. Svatošová designed the "Tribute to Bohumil Hrabal" collage, painting fragments of his writing on the wall, with an enormous portrait, the obligatory typewriter and other memorabilia.

OLD JEWISH CEMETERY FOR PLAGUE VICTIMS

16

Mahlerovy sady, Fibichova, Praha 3
• Open every Monday and Wednesday 11am–3pm, Friday 9am–1pm except on Jewish holidays
• Metro: Namesti Jiřího z Poděbrad; Tram: 11, Náměstí Jiřího z Poděbrad stop

Tomb
of the Golem?

The Žižkov TV Tower dominates the skyline of Mahlerovy sady (Mahler Gardens), formerly a Jewish cemetery for plague victims, only a small part of which is preserved and still accessible to the public.

According to a Prague legend, this is in all likelihood where the Golem was buried.

An old Jewish legend does indeed say that at the time the Golem was overpowered, the Jewish quarter was hit by the plague. On the death of his daughter, one of the ghetto's inhabitants is said to have discreetly placed her body in the coffin with the remains of the Golem, then, with his son, carted the coffin at night to the place now known as Žižkov, where it was secretly buried.

This is where the various legends begin to diverge: in one version, the man and his son arrived at the hill called Židovské pece (Jewish oven); another version says that the Golem was buried in a grave at the cemetery for plague victims, now called Mahlerovy sady.

KRAKONOŠ-RÜBEZAHL SCULPTURE

Čerchovská 11, Praha 2
• Metro: Namesti Jiřího z Poděbrad; Tram: 11, Náměstí Jiřího z Poděbrad
stop

> **Personified**
> **symbol**
> **of sovereign**
> **mountains**

The street leading from Rieger Gardens (Riegerovy sady) to the Žižkov TV Tower is called Krkonošská, after the mountain range on the Czech-Polish border (Krkonoše or "Giant Mountains"). Its legendary ruler was Krakonoš-Rübezahl, a mountain giant, the spirit incarnate of the region, which is why his imposing statue is leaning against the corner of a house at the junction of Krkonošská and Čerchovsk streets.

WHO WAS THE REAL KRAKONOŠ?

The name Rübezahl-Rybrcoul appears in Czech and German folklore from the 15th century onwards, first as a spirit of the mountains and forests and then a demon of the wind, giant and genie. From the 16th century, his earlier name of Rübezahl was used as a term of ridicule.

The Germans devised the name from *Rübe* (beetroot) and *zählen* (to pay) because in many legends Rübezahl paid not with money but with beets. Another etymology gives the source as Lucifer (Devil), which if read backwards spells Repicul.

In *Miscellanea historica regni Bohemiae*, a 1679 treaty by Bohuslav Alois Balbin, a Czech Jesuit, he was described as a ghost sitting on the steep slopes at the peak of Mount Sněžka, swinging his dangling legs and shouting monotonously.

He also sometimes takes the form of a monk, miner, hunter, old man or wild horse, frog, rooster or crow.

Joining the pilgrims, he taught them the secrets of Nature and the mountains, but if insulted he turned into a terrible demon, taking over the natural elements and causing lightning, rain, hail or snow in summer.

People used to go up into the mountains at the source of the Elbe and sacrifice black roosters to him.

Until the mid-17th century, Rübezahl-Rybrcoul was a demonic local figure little known to the Krkonoše people.

After the publication of several tales by J. P. Prätorius (in *Daemonologia Rubenzalii Silesii* of 1662 in three volumes, and *Satyrus Etimologicus* of 1672), stories about Rübezahl began to spread, particularly in Germany, where he was of interest to academics. Writer of fairy tales K. A. Musäus drew upon the work of Pretorius.

Krakonoš, the Czech equivalent of Rübezahl, is a made-up word which from the 19th century replaced Rübezahl in general use.

The name occurred for the first time in V. Hájek's *Kronika česká* (Czech Chronicle) as "Krkonoss", perhaps an allusion to the Ptolemaic Krokontoi, as a geographer of antiquity referred to the Krkonoše – Giant Mountains.

CUBIST DOORWAY OF THE CHURCH OF ST ADALBERT

⓲

U Meteoru
- Tel: 283 892 404
- Open during Mass: Sunday at 10am, Tuesday, Thursday, Friday and Saturday at 5pm
- Metro: Palmovka; Tram: 10, 24, 25, Stejskalova stop

A forgotten Art Nouveau gem

I n the centre of Libeň, near the castle but hidden behind houses, you'll find the stunning Church of St Adalbert (St Vojtěch), a forgotten gem of Czech Art Nouveau architecture.

The wooden church by architect Emil Králíček, built between 1904 and 1905, comes as a great surprise to its infrequent visitors, with its Cubist doorway and strange square tower topped by an onion dome, which rises to 23.7 metres in height.

Intended as a temporary expedient due to lack of funds, the church has finally been preserved for its architectural quality.

NEARBY

Also in Libeň, the pretty Art Nouveau building in Zenklova Street belonging to Sokol (a gymnastics association founded in the 19th century) was also built by Králíček in 1909–10.

BULLET HOLES IN LIBEŇ'S FORMER GAS TANK ⓳

Ke Kouli
- info@vzlu.cz
- Metro: Palmovka; Tram: 3, 8, 10, 12, 15, 24, 25, Palmovka stop

> **A masterpiece of industrial architecture**

Built in the 1930s, Libeň's former gas tank (Libeňský plynojem), with its 270-tonne sphere, 20 metres in diameter, resting on eight sheet-metal legs anchored in a concrete base, is a minor masterpiece of industrial architecture. It is one of the world's last surviving gas-holders where the outer casing has been preserved.

The gas tank, which was in service for ten years, was damaged towards the end of the Second World War: it was strafed from a plane and a grenade smashed through the south side of the tank and exploded inside – fortunately, it was almost empty at the time. Although a section of metal was fixed to the point of impact (on the north side, machine-gun bullet holes can still be seen), the tank could no longer be used for gas, and after further restoration was taken over in 1949 by the Aeronautical Research and Test Institute. The site, home to the largest wind tunnel in the Czech Republic (see below), is still used for scientific research.

NEARBY

LIBEŇ WIND TUNNEL ⓴

Ke Kouli
- info@vzlu.cz • Tel: 602 445 687
- Open during European Heritage Days (EHD) from 7 to 15 September every year
- Metro: Palmovka; Tram: 3, 8, 10, 12, 15, 24, 25 Palmovka stop

For one week a year during European Heritage Days, the largest wind tunnel in the Czech Republic, located in a former gas tank at Libeň, is open to the public.

The tour offers an insight into the operation of a wind tunnel, in which tests are run on scale models of new aircraft, for example. The simulated air speed in the tunnel can attain Mach 2, twice the speed of sound.

CAVE AT TROJA CHÂTEAU ㉑

Praha 7
• Tel: 233 540 741
• Open: Tuesday–Sunday 10am–6pm, Friday 1pm–6pm (gardens until 7pm)
• Bus: 112, Zoologická zahrada stop

I n front of Troja Château a double flight of steps leads to the gardens in the centre of which is a large man-made cavern.

Designed by two sculptors from Dresden, Johann Georg and Paul Heermann, this exceptional site with its mysterious atmosphere is definitely worth a visit. In the depths of the cavern, monumental sculptures symbolise the struggle of the Titans with the ancient gods. Other statues ranged along the terrace balustrade are allegories of the days and seasons as well as different parts of the world.

> *An exceptional and little-known site*

Troja Château is in fact a copy of the beautiful villas around Rome admired by the man who commissioned it, Count Václav Vojtěch of Šternberg, during his travels in Italy. Built between 1678 and 1685, the château was designed by French architect Jean-Baptiste Mathey with the help of Carpoforo Tencalla (who painted the frescoes on the ground floor), Francesco Marchetti and his son Giovanni Francesco (first-floor frescoes) and Flemish painters Abraham and Isaac Godyn (*trompe l'œil* decoration in the central great hall).

The cavern is connected to the vast original cellars which today house a wine bar and museum.

U TROJSKÉHO KONĚ CAFÉ

Vodácká, Trója
- Tel: 777 267 855
- www.utrojskehokone.cz
- info@utrojskehokone.cz
- Open daily 12 noon–8pm
- Bus: 112, Kovárna stop

On the banks of the Vltava River in the Trója district (Czech for Troy), a shrewd owner had the idea of building a huge wooden horse, an astonishing replica of the famous Trojan horse.

This one functions as a bistro where the menu includes wines from local vineyards. The venue is also an art gallery.

*Wine
in a Trojan horse*

The name of the district, Trója, comes from the castle of the same name, whose architect was a great admirer of classical architecture, and the history of the Trojan War in particular (see p. 207).

TROJAN HORSE

The episode of the Trojan horse is one of the most famous of the Trojan War, which raged between the Trojans (in present-day Turkey) and the Greeks. The story is touched upon in Homer's *Odyssey* and recounted in more detail in Virgil's *Aeneid*.

The cause of the war was the abduction of Helen, wife of Menelaus, King of Sparta (Greece), by Paris, a Trojan prince. To punish the Trojans, the Greek kings joined forces and laid siege to Troy. After ten years of siege, the Greeks managed to enter the city through the ruse of the Trojan horse, devised by Odysseus.

The Greeks built a huge, hollow wooden horse and hid a troop of soldiers inside. A Greek spy managed to convince the Trojans to accept this gift, despite the warnings of Laocoon and Cassandra. The horse was pulled inside the walls of the city, where a great feast was held. At night the Greeks emerged from the horse and opened the gates, letting the rest of the army in to loot the city.

PET CEMETERY

U Drahaně
• Open 24/7
• Bus: 102, Staré Bohnice stop

> *A fragment of the Great Pyramid in Prague*

In front of the old graveyard of Bohnice psychiatric hospital, an intriguing pet cemetery was established in the 1990s.

You'll notice the amount of care the owners lavish on the graves of their favourite pets, which often resemble miniature gardens bordered by low painted fences and decorated with a mass of flowers.

Several items stand out among the extraordinary graves and monuments: a post against which a dog has relieved itself, a fragment of the Great Pyramid of Cheops that someone brought back for their dog, and the large tomb of two German shepherds buried along with a pile of tennis balls by their Dutch owner.

ST WENCESLAS CHURCH

Psychiatric Therapeutic Institution Bohnice
Ústavní, Bohnice
• Tel. 284 016 109
• jaromir.odrobinak@plbohnice.cz
• Open during Mass: Monday, Wednesday and Friday at 3.30pm, Sunday at 10am, during European Heritage Days (EHD), 7–15 September every year, and for cultural activities
• Bus: 177, 200, 202, Odra stop

Art Nouveau church in hospital grounds

The Church of St Wenceslas (Václav) in the grounds of Bohnice psychiatric hospital is an Art Nouveau building of outstanding interest, notably for its square tower topped with a dome. Located far from the tourist trails, it is relatively unknown – all the more reason to discover this spectacular ensemble, designed in the years 1911–14 by the architect V. Roštlapil.

The church was deconsecrated in the 1950s and used as a warehouse by a local military unit that ran some of the psychiatric services. Since 1990, it has rediscovered its religious vocation.

DOLNÍ CHABRY

Ládevská 29/542, Chabry, Praha 8
• Bus: 162, 169, 370, 371, 372, 373, 374, 608, Prunéřovská stop

Prague's only menhir

Although in the early 20th century the Chabry menhir (named after a village that became part of Prague in 1968) was still standing in open fields, it is now surrounded by houses.

Incorporated in the front garden of house No. 29/542 on Ládevská Street, near the intersection with Pod Křížem Street, this standing stone ("menhir" comes from the Breton words for stone, *men*, and long, *hir*) is thought to be the only authentic menhir in Prague, although a second stone was recently erected in the same garden. The elevated site might also have been the crossroads of ancient routes to Prague.

Nicknamed "Kamenný slouha" (Valet Stone), perhaps because it recalls the bent silhouette of a man, the menhir is of grey flint with light-coloured veining, girth 2.75 metres and height 1.57 metres.

In the courtyard of the Institute of Archaeology in Malá Strana, Letenská 4 (closed to the public) is a monument that is thought to have been a sightline for the stone circle that used to stand by the village of Libenice, near Kutná Hora.

MENHIRS: PLANETARY ACUPUNCTURE?

Telluric currents, caused primarily by changes in the terrestrial magnetic field, consist of electrical energy flowing through the Earth's crust from a depth of about 100 km. These currents, the subject of scientific study since the 1930s (by Hartmann, Wissman, Peyre and others), rise to the surface along geological faults and underground streams and on emerging from the surface layers are counterbalanced by cosmic rays (mainly from solar radiation). This equilibrium of terrestrial and cosmic energy is essential to human, animal and plant life on Earth. However, when the equilibrium is disturbed, the population of the affected area may experience severe pathological effects (health problems). This is what can happen at a place that naturally gives off "good vibes" or "bad vibes". The instability occurs either when telluric currents are particularly strong at a specific place (above the meeting of underground streams or geological faults, for example) and are no longer "cancelled out"; or on the other hand, in places where the solar radiation is not strong enough to offset the terrestrial radiation. According to certain writers,* the peoples of antiquity intuitively felt these telluric currents and knew how to channel and use them by siting menhirs, dolmens and, more generally, temples or churches at strategic points. Just as an acupuncturist inserts needles at precise points on a person's body, they transformed the telluric energy into subtly beneficial waves and rebalanced a site by diverting the surplus energy into the surroundings.

*Bretagne magique et vibratoire, by Adolphe Landspurg and Norbert L'Hostis, published by Guy Trédaniel, Paris (French only).

MENHIRS IN BOHEMIA

Although most of the world's megaliths or standing stones (from Greek *mega* = large; *lithos* = stone) are in France, they are also found in the United Kingdom, Germany, the Czech Republic and the Caucasus.
There are 26 known menhirs in north-west Bohemia, around the towns of Slaný and Velvaryn, although a few isolated examples are scattered around the country, notably at Drahomyšl, Kamenný Most and Ledce. The tallest stone (3 metres) in Czech territory stands in open fields between the villages of Klobuky and Telce, north-west of Prague. It is claimed that whenever the nearby church bell rings out for the Angelus prayer, the stone moves a step closer to the church: its arrival there will herald the end of the world. Crosses engraved on some menhirs, notably those at the villages of Družec and Sme no, show that they were appropriated by the ecclesiastical authorities.
The menhir nearest to Prague is in the small village of Horom ice.
The most famous alignment of stones in the Czech Republic, poetically referred to as the "Bohemian Carnac", is at Kounov, near the town of Rakovník. Another alignment has been found in the woods near the village of Ne emice.

CONTROL TOWER OF FORMER KBELY AIRPORT

Prague Museum of Aviation and Astronautics
Former Kbely Airport
Mladoboleslavská 1992/148, Praha 19-Kbely
• Open during European Heritage Days (EHD), 7–15 September every year
• Bus: 185, 259, 269, 302, 375, 376, 378, Letecké muzeum stop

> ❝❝ *Controlling the water supply*

The construction of an airfield began in November 1918 on the plateau between the towns of Kbely, Letňany and Vysočany, an ideal site. Several buildings and hangars soon appeared and a month later the first plane took off. This was the first major airport to be built in Czechoslovakia after the First World War, although it became less important in 1937 when Praha-Ruzyne International Airport opened (now Václav Havel Airport Prague).

The control tower, which today dominates the Aviation Museum below, served a dual purpose for almost 80 years: to guide planes in to land and as a water tower.

The 43-metre tower is the work of architect Otakar Novotný, a well-known figure in the 1920s. Jan Lauda ornamented the base with four sculptures on an aeronautical theme.

The lamp on top of the water tower was one of the few navigational

instruments available to pilots at the time. Its powerful French-made reflector has a luminous intensity of 2.75 million candlepower (archaic unit of measurement): its beam could be seen 80 kilometres away in clear weather.

EARLY RADIO STATION
Kbely Airport is connected with the development of radio as well as the history of aviation and space flight. On 18 May 1923 Radio Prague, the largest regular civil broadcaster in Europe after the BBC, began transmitting programmes from the tower roof.

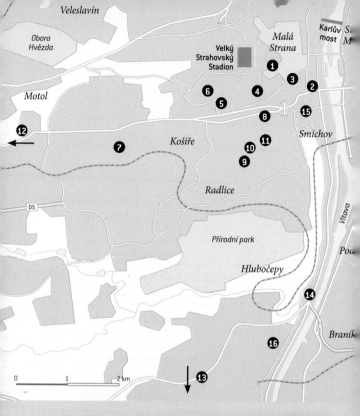

OUTSIDE THE CENTRE - SOUTH

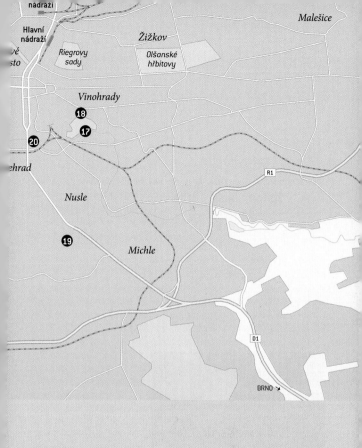

SUNDIAL COLUMN IN KINSKÝ GARDEN ❶

Kinský Garden
Kinského zahrada 98, Praha 5
• Tel: 257 325 766
• Tram: 6, 9, 12, 20; Bus: 176, 510, Švandovo divadlo stop

An astonishing sundial

Within the 22-hectare Kinský Garden (Kinského zahrada), near the lake at the top of the park, stands a remarkable sundial.

The southern face of the sundial (towards the city) contains a niche with a statue of St Roch – whose pilgrim's staff forms the style* that casts the shadow – and the numerals for the hours from 10am to 8pm.

On the eastern face, Christ on the Cross – where the style is the spear piercing his side – shows the hours from 4am to 2pm.

On the western face, a statue of St Rosalia holding roses and lilies (a lily was the original style) shows the hours from 4pm to 8pm.

Finally, on the north-eastern face, St Sebastian with an arrow piercing his

chest (again the original style) marks the hours from 4pm to 8pm.

The orientation of the figures and the hour indicated by each of them were not chosen at random: St Roch, to whom people say prayers to keep the plague at bay, looks to the south side of the city, while to the north St Sebastian offers protection from the plague. So Prague is symbolically protected throughout the day.

Just as Christ symbolises dawn and the daily resurrection of the light, so St Rosalia, with her rose, another symbol of the dawn, is naturally oriented towards the sunrise in the east.

*Style: rod of a sundial casting a shadow that can be projected onto a surface to read the time.

GROTTO-WINDOW
OF PORTHEIMKA SUMMER HOUSE

Štefánikova 12 (Matoušová 9)
• Tel: 604 241 855
• Open daily except Monday 1pm–6pm
• Tram: 6, 9, 12, 20, Arbesovo náměstí stop

*A small
fountain
for birds*

From the garden, you can see a strange construction in place of what appears to be a blocked-up window on the first floor of Portheimka summer house.

Go a little nearer and you'll realise that it's really a small fountain set into in a grotto-like niche, complete with an overflow and waterbasins for the birds that used to nest there.

The grotto, consisting mainly of igneous rocks such as gneiss as well as onyx and agate, is filled with shells and the bones of marine animals and decorated with artificial stalactites.

Now rebuilt and covered with a net, it no longer welcomes birds.

Between 1725 and 1728, the renowned Baroque architect of German origin K. J. Dientzenhofer (who also designed St Nicholas Church in Malá Strana) built his family a summer house that was later renamed Portheimka. On the first floor, the ceiling of the main room features a fresco known as the "Bacanale" by the painter V. V. Reiner, family friend and godfather to the owner's children.

CHURCH OF ST MICHAEL THE ARCHANGEL ❸

Kinského sady
• Tel/Fax: 224 920 686
• Visits by appointment. Also open during Mass on Sunday at 10am and Monday at 8am
• Tram: 6, 9, 12, 20; Bus: 176, 510, Švandovo divadlo stop

I t was in the second half of the 17th century that the superb wooden Orthodox Church of St Michael the Archangel was built in the village of Velké Loučky near Mukachevo (in present-day Ukraine). In 1929 it was dismantled log by log and transported to the heights of Prague's Kinský Garden, where it was reassembled.

A moving church

The church was a gift to the city from the inhabitants of Ruthenia, a region on the borders of Poland, Ukraine, Slovakia, Hungary and Romania – before Ruthenia was annexed by the Soviet Union in 1945, Prague was its capital.

The church is built in Bojkov style, which incorporates popular Baroque elements characterised by three roughly rectangular wooden sections on top of which are wooden towers with shingle-covered roofs and onion domes.

The ensemble stands some 14 metres high and 8 metres wide, although the highest tower rises to over 17 metres.

White, green and red – the three colours that typify the Orthodox religion and symbolise faith, hope and love respectively – are incorporated in the decoration of the towers and the interior.

The building has been used by the Orthodox Church since 2008.

FRESCOES OF THE CHURCH OF ST GABRIEL   ➍

Holečkova, Praha 5 Smíchov
• Open during Mass on Sunday at 11.15am and during European Heritage Days (EHD) from 7 to 15 September
• Bus: 176, 510, Kobrova stop

A rare example of the Beuronese School

Built in neo-Romanesque style in the late 19th century, the Church of St Gabriel is decorated with many frescoes of the Beuronese School, which developed mainly in Germany in the 19th century (see opposite). The frescoes, inspired by ancient Egypt, give surprisingly Egyptian features to the different characters: for example, the Virgin Mary resembles the Egyptian goddess Isis.

Egyptian gods have profoundly influenced Christianity, which in its early days preferred to assimilate existing cults rather than suppress them, in order to be accepted. Thus Christianity incorporated elements of the Mithraic cult (the sun god of Persian origin) as well as from Egypt, whose influence had spread widely throughout classical Greece and the Roman Empire.

Thus, just as Mary remained a virgin, Isis was also impregnated by Osiris without their union. Christian Black Madonnas are also partly based on Isis (see p. 24).

BEURONESE SCHOOL: A LITTLE-KNOWN ART THAT INFLUENCED KLIMT?

The art of the Beuronese School is a mystical monastic style that invites contemplatation and meditation. Characterised by the symmetry and purity of its lines, misty colours, peaceful and serene with a trace of mystery, the Beuronese School was established by the Benedictine monks Desiderius Lenz (1832–1928) and Gabriel Wüger (d. 1892) in the late 19th century at Beuron monastery (Baden-Württemberg, Germany).

Peter Lenz, who was fascinated by the achievements of the Babylonians, Egyptians and Greeks, had received an extensive education in painting as well as architecture before being admitted to Beuron in 1872.

Several monks of this community, such as Lenz, had been artists before taking the cloth (Dutch artist Jan Verkade, born in 1868, was a member of the Nabis – a group of post-Impressionist avant-garde artists in France – before converting to Catholicism and entering Beuron). They began to conceive of religious buildings in a spirit of wishing to revive the art of the early Church.

Lenz was obsessed with geometry and proportions that reflected, according to him, the order willed by God. Seeking to make their art majestic, solemn and hieratic, the artist monks of Beuron worked as a team and in total anonymity: their works are for the glory of God, not the artists.

The fame of the monks grew rapidly – the avant-gardists of the Vienna Secession invited them to their 1905 exhibition. According to some experts, the Beuronese School is even thought to have been a strong influence on Gustav Klimt.

The main achievements of the Beuronese School are found at:

Conception Abbey (Missouri, United States), where two Beuronese monks had emigrated;

Beuron Abbey (Germany), which has the largest monastic library in the country (over 400,000 volumes);

Church of St Gabriel, Prague;

Abbey of St Hildegard (Germany).

TEMPLE OF THE NIGHT AND KNOWLEDGE ⑤

Klamovka Park
Plzeňská, Praha 5-Smíchov
• Park open daily
• The pavilions are open during European Heritage Days (EHD),
7–15 September every year
• Tram: 6, 9, 10, 16, Klamovka stop

> **Masonic building recalling Mozart's Magic Flute?**

Klamovka is a rococo-style property with a splendid public garden on the edge of Smíchov and Košíře districts. It was built on the site of the former vineyards established by Emperor Charles IV near the walls of old Prague. Klamovka is the family name of the counts of Clam-Gallas, who had acquired the property in the mid-18th century.

The design was influenced by the desire to create romantic nooks to cover up the affair between Count Clam-Gallas and singer Josefina Dušková, he being one of her admirers.

Among the many buildings that embellish the park is the beautiful little Temple of the Night and Knowledge, built around 1790, and known as Nebíčko (little heaven or heavens) because of its glazed cupola that features a starry sky. An artificial grotto sits just below.

Some experts have suggested a relationship between this building and Mozart's *Magic Flute* opera, which refers to the ceremonies of Masonic lodges and in which the Temple of Knowledge also appears (in Acts I and II).

In 1787 Mozart invited the Freemasons Franz Josef Anton Thun-Hohenstein and Christian Filip Clam-Gallas to Prague: the first was an eminent member of the Zu Wahren Eintracht lodge in Vienna, and the second was a leading light in Prague Freemasonry. Josefina Dušková might even have sung the Queen of the Night aria from the opera at Klamovka.

The park also has a classical pavilion decorated with a number of Masonic symbols.

THE MAGIC FLUTE, A MASONIC OPERA?

Many people believe that the themes of *The Magic Flute* are taken from the initiation rituals of the Freemasons, to which Mozart and librettist Emanuel Schikaneder belonged, although Schikaneder had been expelled.

The initiatory journey of Tamino and Pamina in Sarastro's temple would thus be inspired by Masonic initiation rites at a lodge.

In his book, *The Magic Flute Unveiled: Esoteric Symbolism in Mozart's Masonic Opera* (published in English by Inner Traditions), music historian Jacques Chailley also explores in detail the musical references to Masonic symbols.

With *The Magic Flute*, Mozart is thus thought to have decided to retrace the great mysteries and finally celebrate the alchemical marriage heralded in the initiatory operas *The Marriage of Figaro*, *Don Giovanni* and *Cosi Fan Tutte*. The composer does seem to have dreamed of resurrecting the lost Egyptian initiation rite, so important to him for world peace, in which women occupied a central place.

HORSE'S HEAD STELE

6

This remarkable stele also found in Klamovka Park was commissioned by Countess Clam-Gallas as a tribute to her favourite horse.

CIBULKA CHINESE PAVILION

Cibulka Park
Plzeňská
• Park open daily, pavilions closed to the public
• Tram: 9, 10, 16, Poštovka stop; Bus: 123, U Lesíka stop

A t Košíře (Praha 5), the Cibulka property is one of Prague's finest examples of late Baroque.

The estate, which had existed since the 14th century, was purchased in 1817 by the Prince-Bishop of Passau, Leopold Leonhard Raymund Reichgraf Joseph Thun-Hohenstein, and given a radical makeover: new plans, including an English park and forest, as well as an artificial ruin, a neo-Gothic forester's house and a hermitage, give it a very appealing romantic style.

One of Prague's finest examples of late Baroque

Not far from the small castle, the Chinese Pavilion is an octagonal pagoda built in 1822.

The current viewpoint, the oldest in Prague, is a 13-metre crenellated tower considered to be the best preserved building on the estate. You reach the top by an external spiral staircase of 76 steps. Above stands the ivy-covered pseudo-Gothic ruin, "Dante's Inferno".

Close by the ruins, within an artificial cave, is a statue popularly known as Škrtíč (the strangler).

GRAVE OF THE "HOLY GIRL"

8

Malá Strana Cemetery
U Trojice, Praha 5-Smíchov
• Book at the Správa pražských hřbitovů offices
• Tel: 251 566 684
• Tram: 6, 9, 10, 16, Bertramka stop

Angel or little girl ?

At the heart of Malá Strana Cemetery, the grave of the "Holy Girl" is an amazing memorial to a moving tale that sees a little girl as an angel.

Anna, born to poor parents in Malá Strana, had a short but unusual life. She could apparently understand the language of birds and animals, and from infancy was considered to possess the soul of a caring angel by everyone she met. When she was three, Anna accidentally fell from a window and was instantly killed.

Her tomb, carved by J. Max, was greatly admired, especially by the children who trooped to see her there.

Baroque architects Christoph and Kilian Dientzenhofer, the Dušek family, owners of Bertramka, and Leopold Thun-Hohenstein are also buried here, in the serene and enchanting atmosphere of this cemetery where most of the graves are covered with creeping ivy.

Founded in 1680 following an outbreak of plague, the Malá Strana Cemetery (Malostranský hřbitov) lies between Smíchov and Košíře. In 1787, following the reforms of Emperor Joseph II, it became the municipal cemetery for the entire left bank of the river (Hradčany, Malá Strana and Smíchov). It was closed in 1884 when there was no more ground left for expansion – it was already surrounded by houses. Subsequently, burials have been carried out at Malvazinky Cemetery.

SUNDIAL IN MALVAZINKY CEMETERY ❾

U smíchovského hřbitova 444/1, Praha 5
• Bus: 137, 501, Malvazinky stop

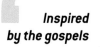

Inspired by the gospels

At the entrance to Malvazinky Cemetery, which opened in 1876, is another extraordinary sundial mounted on a column.

This one consists of four niches featuring statues of Christ (shown twice), the Virgin Mary and St Joseph.

In the north-east niche (an *Ecce Homo* depiction of Christ), the style* takes the form of a reed that casts a shadow on the numerals 4 to 8 of the morning. In the south-east niche, the style is surprisingly enough the spear piercing Christ's side. It casts its shadow on the numerals 4 to 12 of the morning and 1 and 2 of the afternoon.

In the south-west niche, the one with the Virgin, the style is a dagger that casts its shadow on the numerals 10 to 12 of the morning and 1 to 8 of the afternoon.

Finally, in the north-west niche (St Joseph), the style is a lily (symbol of purity and of the saint because he and Mary continued to live chastely after the birth of Jesus) in the hand of the saint which throws its shadow on the

numerals 4 to 8 of the afternoon.

The placement of the figures on the sundial follows the chronological order of the Gospel with, first, the reed that Christ held while Pontius Pilate presented him to the Jews (morning from 4 to 8 on this sundial), then Christ crucified at Golgotha, and finally his death which, according to tradition, occurred at 3 in the afternoon (late morning and numerals 1 to 3 on the dial). The afternoon hours are devoted to the parents of Jesus, but the entire day is under the protection of the Holy Family.

There is a similar sundial in Kinský Garden [see p. 218].

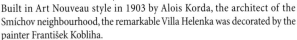

NEARBY

A CORNER OF ENGLAND IN THE HEART OF EUROPE

Prima, Praha 5
• Bus: 137, 501, Malvazinky stop

Near Malvazinky Cemetery, between Přimá and Xaveriova streets, the pre-Second World War workers' housing scheme – the only one in Prague – is reminiscent of small family houses in the English suburbs.

VILLA HELENKA

Na Václavce 30, No. 1078/30
• Bus: 137, 501, Vaclavka stop

Built in Art Nouveau style in 1903 by Alois Korda, the architect of the Smíchov neighbourhood, the remarkable Villa Helenka was decorated by the painter František Kobliha.

Today, you can still see an angel spreading its golden wings on the side façade, high gables embellished with stucco and frescoes, and a sundial in relief surrounding a floral design.

TOMB OF VÁCLAV BABINSKÝ

Řepy Cemetery, Praha 17
Žalanského
• Bus: 225, Řepský hřbitov stop

> ## *The beloved bandit*

The village of Řepy, founded around the 13th century, was joined with Prague in 1968.

Some fine old buildings have survived, such as the Romanesque Church of St Martin and the former women's prison and convent, part of the Church of the Holy Family.

In this convent lived and died the legendary Czech bandit Václav Babinský, who ended his life as a gardener.

In his youth, Babinský made a living by robbery and assault in the forests north of Litoměřice, which soon acquired an accursed reputation. After finally murdering someone, he was arrested in 1835 and charged with a dozen aggravated robberies – although the authorities only had evidence for six of them – and given a 20-year prison sentence.

First sent to Brno, where he served his time in the dark and damp dungeons of Špilberg Castle, Babinský was later transferred to the monastery and penitentiary at Kartouzy (now Valdice) near Jičín, where the Congregation of the Sisters of St Charles Borromeo educated him and made him repent. Now a pious man and model prisoner, he worked as a helper, caring for his sick inmates and looking after the prison garden.

On his release in 1861, the sisters of the Order lodged him near their convent at Řepy, at what is now Žalanského No. 20.

The story goes that in his spare time Babinský loved to go round the Prague pubs, where he related tales from his life in exchange for a beer. He died on 1 August 1879 at the age of 83 and was buried at the Řepy prison cemetery, where his grave – a stone roughly shaped like a menhir – can be found in a quiet corner. It's said that all the nuns wept at his burial.

In the Czech Republic his name is synonymous with robbery, theft and criminality.

OLD LIME KILNS AT VELKÁ CHUCHLE

Pacold Lime Kiln
V Dolích, Praha-Velká Chuchle
• Bus: 244, Velká Chuchle stop

*Lime kilns
like no others*

The old lime kilns at the western end of the village of Velká Chuchle, towards Slivenec, were built around 1890 by Prof. J. Pacold, Rector of the Technical University of Prague.

Technically, these kilns are exceptional in the sense that they could process ungraded limestone, which was mined in a nearby quarry.

More traditional lime kilns are circular and only process graded limestone.

When production ceased before the Second World War, the kilns fell into disrepair until 2004, when they were renovated and classified.

Lime is a white powdery substance obtained by heating limestone, traditionally in a kiln, until it breaks down. It has been used since antiquity as a binding agent in stonemasonry.

Fig. 78. — Four à chaux.

NEARBY

THE LEGENDARY ŠEMÍK'S HOOF PRINTS

According to an old legend, on the left of Zlíchov rock (Praha 5) the hoof prints of the legendary horse Šemík can be seen indented in the ground, after his jump over the ramparts of Vyšehrad citadel during the flight of proud Horymír (see p. 172)

THE HERMIT WHO EXORCISED DEMONS

Prokopské údolí valley, south-west of the city, extends from Nové Butovice to Velká Ohrada and from Barrandov to Hlubočepy. It was designated a nature reserve to protect one of Prague's important natural environments. It covers a karstic and geologically significant territory with strata rich in fossil beds of many species, minerals and grasslands.

The valley is named after the hermit Procope, one of the Czech saints, who lived in a cave there and is believed to have exorcised evil spirits. Svatoprokopská cave, the largest in Prague at 120 metres, was destroyed during the course of limestone mining in the 19th century. It used to be the site of many great pilgrimages. A wooden cross, recently placed near the cave, commemorates this site. A very attractive lake at Hlubočepy was created by the flooding of a former limestone quarry.

MODEL OF PRAGUE

Království železnic (Railroad Kingdom)
Stroupežnického 23, Praha 5, Smíchov
• www.kralovstvi-zeleznic.cz/
• Open daily 9am–7pm
• Metro: Andel; Tram: 6, 9, 10, 16, Andel stop

*Prague
in 1830*

Based on Langweil's model city, another less well-known miniature of Prague was created by Rudolf Šíp between 1965 and 1977 (the year of his death), on a scale of 1:420.

The paper model shows Prague as it was in 1830, with 3,220 buildings, 20 churches, nine synagogues and five towers in the historic centre. It offers a view of the city that no longer exists, showing the banks of the Vltava before its development, St Vitus Cathedral without the characteristic towers that were completed later, and so on.

Stored away for years in warehouses and cellars, the model is now on display at Království železnic (Railroad Kingdom) in the Smíchov district.

There is yet another model of Prague, interactive this time. A system of miniature cameras mounted inside the locomotives gives visitors the chance to imagine riding through the miniature surroundings. On a scale of 1:1000, it covers an area of 115 square metres.

JOACHIM BARRANDE PLAQUE

Barrandov rocks, Zbraslavská
• Tram: 4, 12, 14, 20, Hlubočepy stop

A French scholar who spent years studying rocks

Barrandov, in the south of Praha 5 district on a rocky promontory of the left bank of the Vltava River, is known for its film industry and studios, which are among the largest in Europe.

These 2 kilometres of cliffs form a natural reserve of 11.5 hectares known as Barrandovské skály (Barrandov rocks).

The reserve contains unique examples of Palaeozoic limestone, remarkable Devonian rock formations and palaeontological deposits of trilobites. The rocky massif is named after French scientist Joachim Barrande, who spent several years studying the region's rocks (see opposite). A commemorative plaque measuring 4.8 by 1.5 metres is affixed high on the cliff overlooking the Vltava.

JOACHIM BARRANDE: THE GREATEST PALAEONTOLOGICAL WORK EVER CARRIED OUT BY ONE MAN

Born in France in 1799, Joachim Barrande was educated at the École Polytechnique in Paris. He helped out at scientific conferences during his studies, worked as a civil engineer, in 1826 entered the service of King Charles X as tutor to his grandson Henri (later Comte de Chambord) and after the July 1830 Revolution followed the Bourbon Court into exile.

In this way he discovered Bohemia and was introduced to Czech cultural life. He met the historian František Palacký and Count Kašpar Sternberg, one of the founders of the National Museum of Prague.

After 1840 Barrande began a walking tour through Central Bohemia to map the terrain once covered by a shallow sea. He travelled regularly around the Prague and Beroun region and made many other trips throughout Europe. His main residence was in Prague, and he even employed the mother of poet and writer Jan Neruda as his first housemaid.

In 1846 he published at Vienna and Leipzig the results of his early work, and after some thirty years of research, the first volume of his great work *Système silurien du centre de la Bohême* (Silurian System of Central Bohemia).

In over 6,000 pages and 1,000 lithographic plates, he described more than 3,500 species of fossilized organisms, thus achieving the greatest palaeontological work ever carried out by one man.

At the time of his death, over seven volumes of the encyclopedia had been published, celebrating the richness of Czech Palaeozoic deposits.

Barrande died in 1883 in Lower Austria. Less than a year after his death, the rocks around Prague that he had studied for much of his life were named after him.

Jáchym Barrande.

CAVE IN HAVLÍČEK GARDENS

• Open daily 24/7
• Tram: 4, 22, Francouzská stop; 6, 7, 24, Nádraží Vršovice stop

Charming stone labyrinth popular with lovers

Havlíček Gardens (Havlíčkovy sady) at Grébovka once covered the two properties of Horní and Dolní Landhausky, purchased around 1850 by Prague industrialist Moritz Gröbe.

The architect Antonin Barvitius built a splendid neo-Renaissance villa in the centre of the grounds, where a vast terraced vineyard with wine garden and gazebo were established. Between 1871 and 1888 Gröbe, who was a keen nature lover, had an English-style park constructed on successive levels surmounted by terraces, with retaining walls and connecting

steps, and a boundary wall with several doors set in it.

Gröbe was considered an eccentric character, sitting for hours in the park in solitary meditation. His heirs later opened up the land to horticultural development and rented out the villa.

In front of the monumental cave and artificial rocks in the north-west of Havlíčkovy sady stands a fountain that once featured a reproduction of Neptune.

In the past the whole area underwent major renovation. Although the cave is now extensively damaged, the illusion remains of a charming stone labyrinth with romantic overtones.

MASONIC SYMBOLISM OF THE SQUARE AND COMPASS

In Masonic symbolism, the set-square stands for rectitude, method and law, three principles symbolically supported by the angles of the triangle. In ancient Egypt, the god Ptah was shown with a rule in his hand to measure the Nile floods. So the 24 inch-rule, which features in Masonic Lodges as a working tool and a measure of time, indicates that we should not squander 24 hours a day in idle and selfish pursuits, but that 8 hours should be devoted to meditation, 8 more to work and the remaining 8 to leisure and rest, although the whole time should be applied to the service of humanity.

The compass, one of the principal Masonic symbols, is the emblem of measure and justice. The basic geometric shape that can be drawn with a compass is a circle around a central point. The ultimate solar symbol, the circle (infinity) is consistent with the point (origin of any event or evolution). The relative and the absolute are thus represented by the action of the compass which, for its part, shows duality (the two legs) and unity (where they join). This is why Freemasonry adopted the compass as one of its major symbols and placed it on the altar of the Lodge, enclosing the square to symbolise the macrocosm and the microcosm, above the Holy Book (Bible, Koran, Vedas, etc. according to the religion of the country where the Masons were established). The book suggests the wisdom that illuminates and directs both macrocosm and microcosm, and in particular the Masonic Order.

BAS-RELIEF OF A NAKED CHILD

Šmílovského 2
• Tram: 4, 22; Bus: 135, Jana Masaryka stop

uilt in 1907, the neo-Renaissance house at the corner of Koperníkova and Šmílovského streets has a white bas-relief representing a naked little boy. In his right hand he holds a compass over a drafting table and in his left a T-square.

Masonic symbols of the square and compass

The inset above features a square and compass interlinked to create a Star of David, the hexagram and ultimate Masonic sign.

MICHLE WATER TOWER

Hanusova, Praha 4–Michle
• Metro: Pankrác; Bus: 118, 124, 170, Brumlovka stop

I n Hanusova Street, bordering the Michle and Krč neighbourhoods, stands the Michle water tower, a stunning building topped by a massive copper-roofed drum.

> *One of Prague's outstanding Art Nouveau buildings*

Built in mortarless brick between 1906 and 1907 by the renowned Czech architect Jan Kotěra, it figures among Prague's outstanding Art Nouveau buildings.

Until 1975, the tower brought the waters of the hydroelectric plant at Podoli to the Vinohrady and Vršovice water department: nowadays it is only used as an underground reservoir. However, plans are under way to turn it into a cultural centre.

NEARBY

TWISTED STREET LAMP RECALLS TRAGIC DESTINIES

Folimanka Park - Praha–Nusle
Street lamp under Nusle Bridge
• Tram: 6, 7, 18, 24, Svatoplukova stop

Connecting the New Town with the southern districts of Prague, Nuselský

most (Nusle Bridge) was built in 1973. At 485 metres long, 26.5 metres wide and 42.5 metres high, and towering above the Nusle valley, it's the highest and largest bridge in the city. Because of its height, the bridge has attracted would-be suicides from the earliest days of its construction: between 200 and 300 people have thrown themselves to their deaths in the valley below.

In the 1990s, a guardrail 2.7 metres high was installed to prevent suicide attempts.

In 2011, the sculptor Krištof Kintera installed a modified street lamp in Folimanka Park: twisted at the top and entitled "Of One's Own Volition – Memento Mori", it commemorates the tragic loss of human life.

ALPHABETICAL INDEX

ALPHABETICAL INDEX

NOTES

NOTES

Acknowledgements

To Michel Dineur, translator,

Eva Kosáková · Židovské muzeum v Praze, Monica Šebová · Společnost přátel beuronského umění, Míla Havelková · Národní kulturní památka Vyšehrad, Správa Pražského hradu, Břevnovský klášter, Památník národního písemnictví, letohrádek Hvězda, Národní muzeum (Památník Jaroslava Ježka), Muzeum policie ČR, Poštovní muzeum Praha, Muzeum Stará Čistírna o. p. s., Muzeum pražského vodárenství, Akademický klub 1 LF UK Praha (Faustův dům), Hrdličkovo muzeum člověka UK Praha, Království železnic Praha.

Photography credits:

All photos were taken by **Jana Stejskalová** with the exception of:

Věžník Statue : Ivo Purš

The attic of the Staronová Synagogue: book by Ivan Mackerle Tajemství pražského Golema, Magnet-Press, Prague 1992

Statue of a dead woman: Správa Pražského hradu

All engravings come from Martin Stejskal's personal collection.

Maps: **Cyrille Suss** · Layout design: **Roland Deloi** · Layout: **Stéphanie Benoit** · Translation: **Caroline Lawrence** · Proofreading: **Jana Gough** and **Kimberly Bess**

© **JONGLEZ 2013**

Registration of copyright: October 2013 – Edition: 01

ISBN: 978-2-36195-027-9

Printed in France by Gibert-Clarey

37 170 CHAMBRAY-LES-TOURS